The Bourbons and Begums of Bhopal

The Bourbons and Begums of Bhopal

The Forgotten History

Indira Iyengar

PAPER MISSILE

NIYOGI BOOKS

Published by
NIYOGI BOOKS
Block D, Building No. 77,
Okhla Industrial Area, Phase-I,
New Delhi-110 020, INDIA
Tel: 91-11-26816301, 26818960
Email: niyogibooks@gmail.com
Website: www.niyogibooksindia.com

Editor: K.E. Priyamvada
Design: Shraboni Roy

ISBN: 978-93-86906-38-0
Publication: 2018

Printed at: Niyogi Offset Pvt. Ltd., New Delhi, India

To my mother

Magdaline Bourbon

She was loving and caring,
And brought us up as a good Christian;
A dignified and strong person,
Her memories and blessings remain with us
all the time.

CONTENTS

INSPIRATION

I am the eldest in the family of the Bourbons of India. I feel that it is my duty to write about my family's gallant past—the family that the Mughals appreciated and the Nawab Begums of Bhopal trusted. For three centuries the Bourbons were buried in oblivion. The people are lost and so are their graves. There are rumours and confusion about the location of their last resting places. I am one of the very few who still knows and remembers this important piece of history.

I have read a chapter or two about this famous family of France, elsewhere. These books are listed in the References. My mother's narration of the family was also very interesting, and I feel it needs to find a place in recorded history. My interest also originates from the time when I was working on my Master's thesis: 'Contribution of the Church [India] to the Indian National and Political Life'. I had to visit the Agra's Archdiocese Archives, to read about the history of the Agra Church. Since the priests knew about my family background, they provided me with access to the library that is not open to the general public. There I came across some important historical documents, which shed light on the role of the Bourbons of Bhopal in the development of the state.

I read the letters of the early missionaries and documents that discussed the Bourbon family. They mentioned the Bourbons, including the first Bourbon who came to India and helped the Jesuits from Goa to meet the Mughal Emperor Akbar. The documents referred to Juliana, wife of Jean Philippe de Bourbon, who was the doctor of Akbar's *harem*. The harem consisted of about 5,000 ladies along with Akbar's *begum*s. Juliana had a special bond with these women. The archives contain a treasure trove of Mughal *farman*s (orders), issued in favour of the Jesuit missionaries. My thesis work further drew my interest towards the Bourbons of India. They were among the Mughals' most trusted men. Since they were neither Hindus nor Muslims, they were viewed as unbiased and extremely loyal.

The purpose of writing this book is to make the famous Bourbons alive once again. People should know about their heroic deeds and the role they played in shaping Bhopal and its history. I was born in Bhopal, in 1939, and love my beautiful city of lakes. I spent the majority of my life in this beautiful Indian city. I want people to know more about the rich history and heritage of Bhopal. Most importantly, I want to share some stories about the women of Bhopal who were very brave and liberal, perhaps unusually so for their time. It was common to find noble women in Bhopal riding horses, sword-fencing and ruling the state.

Through this book, my hope is to relive the contribution that my family had made to the history of Bhopal. The Begums of Bhopal appointed the Bourbons to key positions in the state adminstration. As a result, Bhopal, which was a princely state, after signing a treaty with the British East India Company in 1818, developed as a peaceful realm with a cosmopolitan culture that merged with India in 1949. In this age where minorities feel threatened, I want to share instances of the liberal attitude of the erstwhile rulers of Bhopal, which is much needed in this time.

This book is a tribute to my mother and a historical account with a personal flavour.

Indira Iyengar

FOREWORD

I have read this book from cover to cover. It is certainly a painstaking effort by the author, Indira Iyengar, whose mother Magdaline was a descendant of the Bourbons of India. The book is a compilation of the authors' memories of her childhood and stories narrated by her mother. Through this book, she wishes to fulfil a promise made by her to her mother, Magdaline Bourbon. The author starts by saying that she is not a historian, but the book provides a strong evidence of her research into the history of the Bourbon family.

The first chapter narrates the arrival of the Bourbons in India, especially the arrival of Jean Philippe de Bourbon. The chapter describes his departure from France and the stories related to his travel to India. Jean Philippe de Bourbon's position in Akbar's court and his marriage with Lady Juliana is also discussed. This also brings up the interesting dynamics of the Mughal Emperor Akbar married to an Armenian doctor, who was Lady Juliana's sister. The Armenians and the Christian Jesuits in Akbar's court are said to had a deep impact on Akbar's secular beliefs. The chapter further discusses Jean Philippe de Bourbon's son, Alexander, who was in-charge of the seraglio and a companion to Akbar's son, Jahangir. Jean Philippe and his wife helped to build the first church of Agra in 1588, where they are buried.

The second chapter deals with the arrival of the Bourbon family in Narwar and Shergarh with many other Christians, including the Armenians. Francis Bourbon, the son of Anthony Bourbon, was the last man to hold charge of the imperial seraglio when Nadir Shah ransacked Delhi in 1758. However, Anthony Bourbon managed to narrowly escape with his family. He took refuge with his family in the Fort of Shergarh, with 300 men and women. The family again faced a massacre by the ruler of Narwar in 1769 and only Salvador, his mother and three children were able to flee.

The third and the fourth chapters form the core of this book, where Bhopal's history is well documented from the earliest times of the Parmar rule and the construction of Sabha Mandal by Rani Shyamli as the University. The history of Bhopal is more broadly narrated to provide the context in which the Bourbons arrived and flourished. The chapter includes mention of the previous rulers of Bhopal such as Nizam Shah and Dost Muhammmad Khan to Manji Mamola, the wife of Nawab Yar Muhammad Khan. It was Manji Mamola who helped Salvador to settle down in Bhopal in 1785. From this point onwards Salvador and his son Balthazar became prominent figures and played a very important role in the history of Bhopal. They both helped to save Bhopal from the Maratha aggression by fighting alongside Wazir Muhammad Khan, Nazar Mohammad Khan and Nawab Ghous

Muhammad Khan. Finally, Balthazar alias Hakim Shahzad Masih played an important role in the Treaty of Raisen in 1818. Shahzad Masih supported Nawab Qudsia Begum to first become the ruler of Bhopal and subsequently ran her state affairs as the Prime Minister of Bhopal. Shahzad Masih's wife Dulhan Sahib lived a long life as a trustworthy and close confidant of the Begums of Bhopal. She spent quite some time with Nawab Qudsia Begum, then with Nawab Sikandar Jahan Begum. She was probably the only lady *Jagirdar* apart from the Nawab's family. She, along with her son Sebastian, served Sikandar Jahan Begum during the Uprising of 1857. The Bourbon family was very well accepted by the Bhopalis and always remained close to the royal family. They were of French descent, yet Bhopali at heart.

Anther important contribution of this book is the family tree or *shajrah* prepared exclusively to complement the research on the Bourbons. This is to my knowledge, the only up-to-date exhaustive family tree line on the Bourbon family in India. The family tree provides the complete family history of the Bourbons of India, which is a major contribution of the book. The family tree is a compilation of family resources, archival documents and previous research papers. The author also used the website Ancestry.com and other sites to gather facts such as dates and relations. Finally, the book also contributes through the use of authentic photographs that date back to the early 18th century. The photographs passed on to her through her family lineage provides a glimpse of the rich family history of the Bourbons.

Some of the photos were taken from historical records and previously published books that depict glimpses of ancient Bhopal.

This book fills a huge gap in the literature regarding the contribution of the Bourbons in Bhopal's history. It provides a compelling case to attribute the success of the Bhopal State to the Bourbons. The narration beautifully situates the contribution of the Bourbons with the description of Bhopal's history during that era. This book is worth reading, as it provides details about the Bourbons of India which have not been shared with a wider audience so far. I wish all the success to the author as she has put in tremendous effort to craft this magnificent book.

Rizwan Uddin Ansari

Historian, Bhopal

PROLOGUE

Magdaline Bourbon, Daughter of Gasper Bourbon
Source: Author's private collection

I am no historian, but I have a story to tell. These are a compilation of the stories narrated to me by my mother, a descendant of the Bourbons. Sometimes in life, one wants to know about our ancestors. The biggest mistake the Bourbons made was not to write about their life or lineage. If only the Bourbons of India, had written their history; generations would have benefited. Today the Bourbons are trying to find their roots. I am probably the oldest in my family who can narrate at least some part of this history. This story is about the French Bourbon who travelled to India, met the Mughal Emperor Akbar and served in his court. His descendants later travelled to Bhopal with their families.

The majority of this book is an account of the French Bourbons who lived in Bhopal, the city where my mother and I were born. I still remember the times when my mother and her four daughters, including me, along with our household help, sat around the fireplace in our house and listened to my mother's stories. My mother had beautiful memories of her childhood in Bhopal, about the women in Bhopal and their multiple valiant accounts and of her father—one of the Bourbon men. There are four versions of the history of the Bourbons in India. The first is written by missionaries, the second by British political agents in India, the third by travellers and adventurers and the fourth by family members. These stories of the Bourbon family are scattered over many documents, some are travelogues, others are historical accounts, but there is no one source to narrate a complete story. In all of these, the common convergence of the origin is that there was a person by the name of Jean Philippe de Bourbon, who arrived in India in 1560, and made his way to the Mughal Emperor Akbar's court, in Agra. He was very distinguished, intelligent, handsome, and seemed to have royal origins. In this book I have tried to compare a number of sources such as descriptions by various historians, Government of India documents such as the *Imperial Gazetter of India*, and also my mother's own account.

Mumtaz Baig, Archivist of National Archives Bhopal, with Indira Iyengar
Source: Author's private collection

I have personally researched in the Archives of the Cathedral of Agra and have compiled documents from the National Archives of India, which are about 500 pages, untouched for 2 centuries. Due to their age, these pages are delicate and would crack with the slightest of pressure. My mother Magdaline's accounts form the backbone of this book. Her photographs included in this book narrate her part of the story as well. Unfortunately the Bourbons never documented their contribution to the Bhopal state nor do we have any written account of their lifestyles. This book is an attempt to do so. The narration of the book includes battles being fought, espionages being sabotaged, romance, poetry, the protagonist being poisoned, royal lifestyles and much more. I have narrated historical episodes along with giving detailed accounts of their lives to know who these foreign travellers were and what their lifestyle was.

Magdaline Bourbon at her wedding with Satish Ghosal
Source: Author's private collection

My mother, Magdaline Bourbon, born in 1903, was the daughter of Gasper Bourbon and the grand-daughter of Bonaventura Bourbon. She often spoke about how the first Bourbon came to India. She knew where her ancestors were buried. She had heard these stories from her father. Her stories also matched other historians whom I have quoted in this book. Magdaline herself looked like a foreigner. She was tall, fair, and had delicate features. It was a rare fusion of oriental and western cultures. The Bourbons were generally very educated, spoke good English and were sincere towards the Royal family of Bhopal.

The Bourbons in India descended from Jean Philippe de Bourbon who was the natural son of Duke Charles III de Bourbon (1489–1527) called 'Connétable de Bourbon'. According to the account given by Sir John Malcolm (Malcolm 1824), the history of this French family in India starts during the Mughal Emperor Akbar's reign. This is when a European named Jean Philippe de Bourbon arrived at the Mughal court in Delhi around 1560. He claimed to be a descendent of one

Bottom Left: Dancers in the court of Bhopal, 1866
Source: Rizwan Uddin Ansari, Historian, Bhopal

Bottom Right: Muharram in Bhopal
Source: Author's private collection

of the noblest French families (Rousselet 1975). Jean Philippe de Bourbon is said to have married Juliana, the sister of Akbar's Christian wife. The Bourbons continued to live in India ever since. Rousselet (1975) states that Jean Philippe de Bourbon left behind two sons: Alexander, born around 1550 and Seville (Charles), born about 1560. Their ancestors travelled to other parts of India and finally came to Bhopal.

Bhopali Lady
Source: Author's private collection

The Bhopal story started with Mamola Bibi, consort of Dost Muhammad Khan, who welcomed Salvador Bourbon in the 1750s. Salvador repaid his due by

Mullahs of Bhopal, 1866
Source: Author's private collection

being loyal to the state. Bourbons who came to Bhopal accepted Muslim names, clothes, language and ultimately settled down in Bhopal. After

Salvador, his son Balthazar Bourbon alias Shahzad Masih (or the Christian Prince) helped to rule the state. It was because of Balthazar Bourbon that a Muslim lady, Qudsia Begum, of the royal family could get the courage to remove her veil and rule the state. Qudsia Begum or Queen Qudsia ruled for many years with the help of Balthazar. After Balthazar, his wife Isabella Bourbon alias Madam Dulhan was responsible for taking care of 500 Christian families in Bhopal, some of who were the descendants of the Bourbons.

My mother, Magdaline Bourbon, was born and raised with the Muslim royal family in Bhopal. She often spoke about her life in the Bourbon Palace (Shaukat Mahal), built for the Bourbons by the Bhopal royal family. Bourbon Prime Ministers left their mark on the French-influenced architecture in Bhopal. The Bourbons are also known for their culturally diverse living style. They went to church, but just like the Muslims the women sat behind a long curtain. They wore Muslim garb and celebrated both Hindu and Muslim festivals. The Bourbon men were great administrators and were very brave. Balthazar Bourbon, was multifaceted, a prolific writer and a linguist. He was well versed in Urdu, Persian, English and Farsi. His collection of Urdu poetry is called *Fitrat*. Some of his works are documented in this book. Bhopal was famous for its poetry sessions or *mushaira*s. Balthazar used to attend those *mushaira*s along with various dignitaries and state officials, including the Royal family. Balthazar was a regular feature in these parties and his poetry was well respected and liked by everyone. It is

Women of Bhopal meeting during the Satyagraha movement near the Unani Shifa Khana in the latter half of the 1940s
Source: Author's private collection

remarkable that the descendant of a Frenchman could recite Urdu and Farsi poetry at night and work as a Prime Minister during the day. The strong bond between the Begums and the Bourbons continued even after Balthazar's demise. The Bourbon family in multiple accounts helped the Begums (ruling queens) by foiling serious plots against them.

This book narrates the history and lifestyle of the Bhopal Bourbons who in many ways shaped the history of Bhopal. The book accounts for multi-cultural aspects of Bhopal, glimpses of which can be seen in the city even now. The contribution of this book is to highlight a forgotten aspect of history, which is the contribution of the Bourbons to Bhopal's history. But it also highlights the secular ways of living as depicted in the architecture, clothes, language and the style of celebrating festivals by Hindus, Muslims and Christians in Bhopal. The book

Islamnagar Fort (Rani Mahal) where Balthazar used to meet Qudsia Begum, who was accepted as Regent and Sikandar Jahan Begum became the ruler in 1819
Source: Author's private collection

carries original photographs from the past, which are rare and have not been disclosed to the public before. These photographs belonged to my mother and have been passed on to me. This book will be a unique gem that combines historical facts with the inter-cultural aspects of Bhopal in earlier times.

ARRIVAL OF JEAN PHILIPPE DE BOURBON IN AKBAR'S COURT

Early Account of the French in India

India has seen many voyagers sail to its ports over the past centuries. Malleson (1984) argues that French voyagers probably first landed in India during the reign of Louis XII in the 1500s. In the year 1503, two ships lured by the idea of profitable trade are known to have sailed to the Eastern seas, but both were lost at sea. The successor of Louis XII, King Francis I, ordered long voyages in 1537 and 1543. King Francis' reign was characterized by war and unrest, so there is no proof that either voyage ever happened (Malleson 1984). We do know, however, that an official French expedition sailed from Le Havre in the first half of the 16th century, but it too was lost at sea.

Earliest French expedition to India
Source: Author's private collection

Fanthome (1895) cites an article by Colonel Kincaid of the Indian Political Service in *The Asiatic Quarterly Review* of January 1887, in which he wrote that a successful voyage to India took place in the latter half of the 16th century (1560 AD). This voyage was under the command of John Philippe de Bourbon of Navarre, who was a member of the younger branch of the family tree of King Henry IV. John Philippe sailed for Madras, India, when he was forced to leave France after a killing related to a family feud. In 1604, a Company was granted letters patented by King Henry IV, but the project failed. Fresh patents were issued in 1615, and two ships were sent to India; only one returned. Voyages continued under the peaceful reign of Henry IV. On 1 June 1604, a Company was established, mainly for trade purposes (Malleson 1984). Seven years later, the Company was renewed under Louis XIII, but the Company did not come into action until 1615 because of disputes among the proprictors and the paucity of funds. In 1616, Commodore de Nets and Captain Antoine Beaulieu voyaged to 'the Indies,' meeting Dutch opposition at Java. More unsuccessful voyages occurred in 1619, when three more ships sailed toward Java.

The French 'Compagnie des Indes' was formed under the auspices of Richelieu and reconstructed under Jean-Baptiste Colbert. They sent an expedition that reached a location between India and France, Madagascar, in 1662. In 1664, the French Compagnie des Indes gained strength in terms of capital acquisition. From Madagascar, some proceeded to India, while others stayed in small islands called the

Isles of France and Bourbons (later renamed the Isles of Mauritius and Reunion), located a little to the east of Madagascar. In 1667, the French Compagnie des Indes sent out a new expedition, under the command of Francois Caron, which reached Surat in 1668 and established the first French factory in India. In 1667 another expedition sailed to Madagascar, found the French colonies to be in a deplorable state, and decided to proceed to the familiar trade location of Surat. Caron was nominated Director-General of French commerce in India.

An expedition thereafter brought an adventurous Bourbon to India. It is said that the Bourbons in India descended from Jean Philippe de Bourbon, natural son of Duke Charles III de Bourbon (1490–1527), called 'Connétable de Bourbon'. The Connétable married Suzanne de Bourbon in 1521; she was a granddaughter of the King of France, Louis XI. Jean Philippe's is an interesting story. As a child, he was obliged to hide himself in the south of France, at Pau, because his father was hated and persecuted by Louise de Savoy and King Francis I in 1527. He remained there for 10 years. As a young man, at the age of 16, Jean Philippe had to escape from France because he killed a French lord in a duel.

The earliest account of Jean Philippe de Bourbon is by Madame Dulhan Bourbon, wife of Balthazar Bourbon, in the form of the following testimony made to a British General named Malcolm. A European named Jean de Bourbon arrived at the court of Delhi during Akbar's reign in 1559. The European claimed to be the descendant of one of the noble families of

France (Rousselet 1975). Turkish pirates had taken Jean Philippe de Bourbon as a prisoner when he was about 16 years old. He disembarked in Egypt as a slave but later became an officer and went to Ethiopia on a mission. Taken prisoner by the Ethiopians, Jean Philippe de Bourbon succeeded in escaping Ethiopia to go on to India.

Other sources confirm the royal background of Jean Philippe de Bourbon, though there is still debate about the actual year of his entry into India. He probably arrived in India circa 1547, though Fanthome (1895) states that he arrived in 1560 and Madame Dulhan Bourbon had claimed 1559. Ram Babu Saksena, in his book *European & Indo-European Poets of Urdu and Persian* includes a description of Jean Philippe by Father Noti S. J., who resided in Bombay. A document purporting to be an Urdu translation of a Persian statement was presented to the Mughal ruler Jahangir in 1605 or 1606 by Jean Philippe, who must have been very old, approximately age 85. In this document, Jean Philippe states that he was the son of the famous Charles Connétable de Bourbon and that his mother died shortly after his birth. He added that he escaped from Rome after the Connétable's death by arranging a mock funeral of himself and, after adventures amongst the Turks, came to India. Father Noti also had documents stating that John Philippe's wife was an Abyssinian princess who bore the name of Magdaline. He adds that, in India, the Mughal Emperor Akbar had made the Bourbon Raja of Shergarh. Father Noti's records suggest that Jean Philippe was still alive in 1606, and that he had two sons: Alexander, born about 1550, and Saville (Charles), born about 1560. According to Father Noti's record, Jean Philippe arrived in India in 1560. Father Noti's investigations have not been published, to date. According to my mother, Magdaline Bourbon, a certain priest from Bombay did possess Bourbon family records, but she used to say that those records were lost with time.

The Bourbons and the Mughal Emperor Akbar

The Bourbons were very impressive and able to attract the attention of the great Mughal emperor Akbar. With their gallant behavior and pleasant demeanor, they navigated difficult circumstances very well. In their honor, it is written:

Khule asman mai Naksh banainge
They will make an impression under the open sky
Waqt ko waqt ke saath chalna sikhaenge
They will teach time to walk with time.

R. V. Smith elaborates that Jean Philippe was given an army post under Akbar. Jean Philippe de Bourbon was tall, fair, and handsome. He had good knowledge of court discipline and decorum. He easily impressed Akbar with his polite mannerisms and family lineage of the French Bourbons. These factors, also present in his descendants, later impressed the Begums of Bhopal, as well. *Le Rajah Bourbon,* a book written by Prince Michael of Greece, states that the Bourbons of India had accumulated a great deal of wealth over many years of service to the Mughals and the Begums

Detail from the *Akbarnama* showing Akbar in the Ibadat Khana; two Jesuit priests are sitting to the left
Source: Author's private collection

of Bhopal. Akbar decided to get Jean Philippe married to a lady known as Bibi Juliana. Some say she was Armenian, though Smith was of the opinion that she was a Portuguese doctor who looked after Akbar's harem. The Armenian scholar Mesrovb Jacob Seth writes that lady Juliana is believed to have been a sister of one of Akbar's Armenian wives, and was a doctor in the royal harem of Akbar.

Jean Philippe de Bourbon was given a *jagir* (land grant) as a gift from Akbar for his performance in the army. He became Raja of Shergarh and his wife Juliana was a well-known figure in Delhi. Maclagan notes that Juliana and her sons owned 'Juliana Sarai and other places near Delhi' (Maclagan 1932, 167) which were granted to her by Aurangzeb and Bahadur Shah. It is said that the land where the current Convent of Jesus of Mary stands was also donated by Juliana's sons. In the memoirs of the Asiatic Society of Bengal, Rev. Hosten (1916) mentions that the Jesuits first gained Akbar's favours by means of a certain Signora Juliana of Goa who was, a 'Lady Doctor' in Akbar's seraglio.

Juliana and Jean Philippe de Bourbon helped to build the first Catholic church in Agra; it was completed in 1588. The land was a gift from the Mughal Emperor Akbar. Two eminent Catholics, Khwaja Martins and Mirza Sikandar Junior, contributed generously toward the extension of this church. The Agra Episcopal archives hold records regarding the construction of this church. One document (date unknown) reads 'the old church [at Agra] was built by Philip Bourbon of the house of Navarre and his wife Juliana, an Armenian lady who was in medical charge of the Emperor's harem.' Father Felix also writes in his memoirs, *The history of John Philip Bourbon de Navarre . . . the Jesuit Missions and the Story of Dona Juliana Dias da Costa* that a note in the Agra mission archives states that the old church [of Agra] was built by Philip de Bourbon of the House of Navarre and his wife Juliana, an Armenian lady, who was in medical charge of the emperor's harem (Felix 1918, 1–53).

In 1610, the three Royal Princes, nephews of the Emperor Jahangir, came to this church to be baptised by Rev. Fr. Corsi, S. J. and Fr. Xavier S. J. The Begum Joanna Samru, popularly known as Begum of Sardhana was also baptised here, according to undated documents from the Agra Archdiocese.

Records of the Agra archdiocese speak of Juliana and Jean Philippe's graves being inside the church compound. However, the graves of Jean Philippe and Juliana were never found. Shah Jahan defeated the Portuguese in 1634 and brought 4,000 Christian prisoners to Agra. In 1634 he released a few Jesuit Fathers on the condition that they dismantle the church, which they did. However, in 1636 Shah Jahan allowed the Fathers to rebuild it. On 8 September 1636, the first Holy Mass was celebrated in this reconstructed Church.

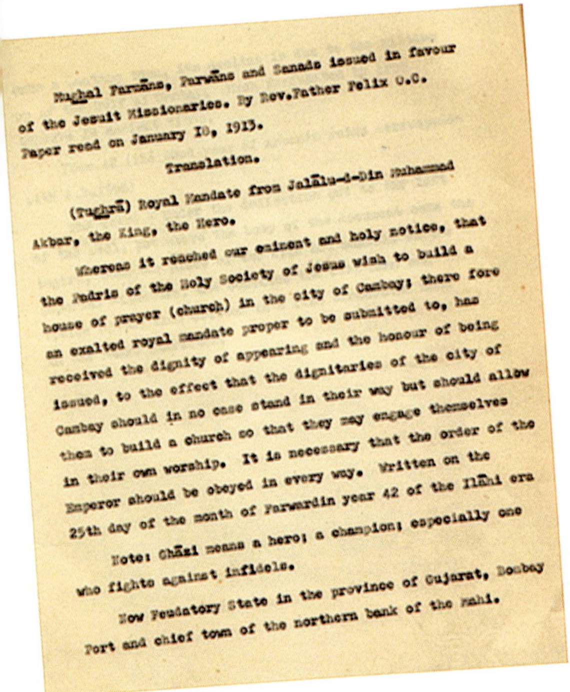
Mughal Farmāns, Parwāns and Sanads issued in favour of the Jesuit Missionaries. By Rev.Father Felix O.C. Paper read on January 10, 1913.

Translation.

(Tughrā) Royal Mandate from Jalālu-d-Din Muhammad Akbar, the King, the Hero.

Whereas it reached our eminent and holy notice, that the Padris of the Holy Society of Jesus wish to build a house of prayer (church) in the city of Cambay; there fore an exalted royal mandate proper to be submitted to, has received the dignity of appearing and the honour of being issued, to the effect that the dignitaries of the city of Cambay should in no case stand in their way but should allow them to build a church so that they may engage themselves in their own worship. It is necessary that the order of the Emperor should be obeyed in every way. Written on the 25th day of the month of Farwardin year 42 of the Ilāhi era

Note: Ghāzi means a hero; a champion; especially one who fights against infidels.

Now Feudatory State in the province of Gujarat, Bombay Port and chief town of the northern bank of the Mahi.

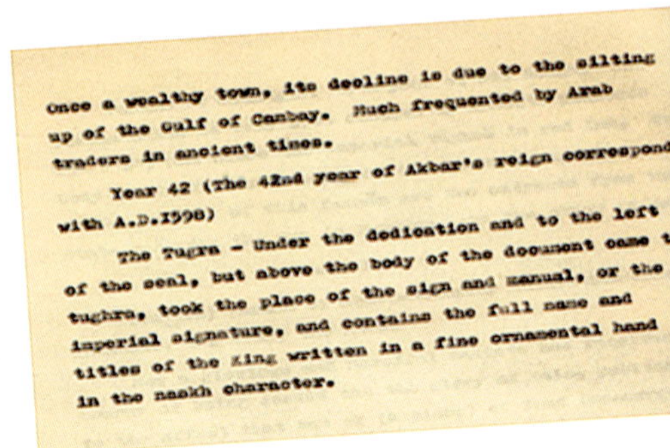
Once a wealthy town, its decline is due to the silting up of the Gulf of Cambay. Much frequented by Arab traders in ancient times.

Year 42 (The 42nd year of Akbar's reign corresponds with A.D.1598)

The Tugra - Under the dedication and to the left of the seal, but above the body of the document came th tughra, took the place of the sign and manual, or the imperial signature, and contains the full name and titles of the King written in a fine ornamental hand in the naskh character.

Akbar's *farman* translated in English, kept in the Archdiocese of Agra Source: Author's private collection

In 1761, the Persian invasion under Ahmed Shah Abdali shattered the declining Mughal empire. During the siege of Agra, Persian soldiers ransacked the church. In 1769, Walter Reinhardt, then Commander of Agra Fort, helped Father Wendel S. J. to rebuild it and make an extension. In 1835, Bishop Pezzoni, with generous aid from Sir John Baptiste Filose, extended the church westward.

Later, the church had other benefactors. Mr John Baptiste Filose provided monetary support to make it Agra's Cathedral. He and his sister, Miss Filose, lived in Gwalior. On Dussehra day, it was a tradition with the Scindia family (rulers of Gwalior at that time) to lead a large public procession. The ruler, Jiwaji Rao Scindia sat on an elephant in the parade. To honor Mr Filose, he was always given an elephant to ride alone. He also had a very honourable position at the Scindia court. Mr Filose and his family in Gwalior had the same stature as the Bourbons in Bhopal. My mother used to visit them often and they used to come to our house in a buggy (a carriage drawn by horses), which was rare during those times. They were the godparents of my younger sister, Susheila Ghosal (the third daughter of Magdaline Bourbon).

Jean Philippe de Bourbon died at Agra in 1592, leaving behind two sons Alexander and Saville; (please see the Bourbon family tree for more details). Alexander was later in charge of Akbar's seraglio, and was a friend and adviser of Emperor Jahangir. Not much is known of his direct descendants. Saville Bourbon (also spelt Seville and Saveille in some records) was born in 1560 and was married to Allemaine in 1582. Saville's son, Alexander Bourbon, was born in 1605 and married a Miss Robertson in 1640. His eldest son, Anthony Bourbon, married the granddaughter of Yakub Khan, of the ruling house of Afghanistan who had converted to Christianity. Yakub Khan held a high post in Delhi with the title of Nawab. Francis Bourbon, the son of Anthony Bourbon, was born in 1680. In 1710, he married an Armenian girl, probably one of his relatives. He was the last man to hold charge of the

The church built on land gifted by Akbar in Agra; outside and inside views
Source: Author's private collection

imperial seraglio when Delhi was sacked in 1737 and he narrowly escaped with his family. He took refuge with his family in the Fort of Sirgarh; they numbered 300 men and women (Saksena 1941, 197). Francis Bourbon II (1718–1778) was said to be a Prince Sovereign of Sirgarh, now known as Shergarh, not far from Narwar.

The Armenians and the Bourbons during Akbar's rule

Buland Darwaza in Fatehpur Sikri
Source: Kuntal Guharaja (commons.wikimedia.org)

Akbar was popular for his secular beliefs and his eagerness to learn from all religious faiths. His tolerance for other religions is also noticeable in his marriages to women of various faiths, most notably Jodha Bai, a Hindu daughter of the House of Jaipur. Akbar also married a Christian by the name of Maria Zamani Begum or Marium Makani Begum. Miriam is critical to the Bourbon story because the family maintains that Juliana was the sister of Akbar's Christian wife, Miriam. Miriam is said to have had her own chapel in one of Akbar's palaces at Fatepur Sikri Fort, 25 kilometers from Agra. Akbar's regard for Christianity is visible in the Buland Darwaza, a large gate structure at the city of Fatehpur Sikri, on which he had transcribed the Quranic inscription: 'Isa [Jesus], son of Mary, said: This world is a bridge, pass over it, but build no houses on it. He who hopes for an hour may hope for eternity. The world endures but an hour. Spend it in prayer, for the rest is unseen.' (source: Personal communication with Shri Mohammad K. K., Director of Archeological Survey of India).

Akbar with Mariam-uz-Zamani Source: en.wikipedia.org/wiki/Mariam-uz-Zamani

In 1949, when my family moved to Agra, we used to take visitors to see Mughal monuments. One of the main sites was Fatehpur Sikri Fort. I still remember an old tourist guide pointing us to a wall on which a faint picture of the mother of Jesus was painted. He used to describe it as the house of Akbar's Christian wife, Mariam Zamani. Another Mughal monument in Agra is the Sikandra, which is the tomb of Akbar. Opposite Sikandra lies the grave of Mariam Zamani. Outside the tomb, a board erected by the Archaeological Survey of

India reads: 'Mariam Zamani was the daughter of Raja Bharmal Kachhwaha of Amer Jaipur and married to Akbar in 1562 A.D. This is controversial because Mariam is the name of Jesus's mother and Zamani is a typical Armenian name.

Seth confirms this claim; he says:

> 'I was completing the proof-reading of my paper "Mirza Zul-Qarnain, a Christian Grandee under three Great Mughals, with Notes on Akbar's Christian wife and the Indian Bourbons" [issued by the Asiatic Society of Bengal]. I also draw my conclusion that Akbar did indeed marry a Christian lady of Armenian origin from an unexpected discovery of a European style painting. It represents Akbar with a Christian girl in partly European attire and the Persian superscription *'Jalal-ud-din Akbar ma Maryam Zamani Begum'* ('Jalal–ud–din Akbar with Maryam Zamani Begum").' (Seth 1897, 152)

Fanthome, also states, 'I have in my possession information which leads me to believe that there is a great deal of truth in the assertion that Akbar had a Christian wife whose name was Miriam.' (quoted in Seth 1897, 152) Father Houston's writing with the photographic illustration of the painting was published in *The Statesman* on 14 November 1916. De Laet, who wrote *The Empire of the Great Mughals* in 1631, just 26 years after the death of Akbar, describes the palace as, 'one set belonging to Mary Makany wife of Akbar'. (Seth 1897, 151) Henry Blochmann, in his translation of the *Ain-I-Akbari,* mentions in a note that there is not the least doubt of 'Akbar having an Armenian wife'. (Seth 1897, 152) Rousselet confirms this claim in *India and its Native Princes,*

Tomb of Mariam-uz-Zamani
Source: Author's private collection

'Near Akbar's mausoleum beyond the enclosure, stands a vast ruined cenotaph enclosing the tomb of the Emperor's Christian wife, the Begum Mariam Zamani.' (quoted in Seth 1897, 152).

Seth, in the *Armenians in India from the Earliest Time to the Present Day*, writes that Akbar had a Christian wife who was an Armenian lady from the banks of the Aras and her name was Miriam, which is the Armenian nomenclature for Mary. He continues that she had Eastern or European features. Seth mentions that he unexpectedly discovered a painting in the European style of art. Representing Akbar with a Christian girl in what appears to be European attire. Fr. Houston's paper with the photographic illustration of the painting was published in *The Statesman* on 14 November 1916. The picture given here is said to have close resemblance to the referenced painting. Seth writes that the picture of Mariam Zamani was brought by Mr A. Stephen, of Camac Street Calcutta, from the estate of the late Prince Muhammad Baktiyar Shah of the house

Akbar's Armenian wife wearing a cross
Source: http://gethashtags.com/photo/11837964427684065_595491367

of Tipu Sultan, who died at Agra in 1855 and lies in the old Armenian Cemetery. Various other characteristics of the picture seemed to favour this view. The picture has been the source of controversy since most people believe that she was a Hindu. However, in this picture Mariam is seen wearing a cross.

The Armenian cemetery at Agra

'The Martyrs Graveyard' in Agra is centuries old. It is now run by the Archeological Survey of India. Due to age, most of names written on the graves are illegible, but this graveyard is the oldest Christian graveyard in Northern India.

Christian Cemetery in Agra
Source: Author's private collection

Top: Grave of Anthonia Bourbon in the Martyrs Graveyard at Agra. She lived a 100 years

Middle: The Martyrs Graveyard in Agra with graves of the Bourbons

Bottom: Tombs of Christians in the Martyrs Graveyard at Agra
Source: Author's private collection

Tombs of the Bourbons in Agra

During my research in 1967 at Agra, I was given special privilege to use the Archdiocese archives. Very few people know of this great wealth of knowledge, which includes documents written by Father Felix in 1913 and documents from the Asiatic Society of Bengal. Father Felix conducted research at the cemetery at Agra, where the graves of Europeans, mostly French and Portuguese people, can be found. Seth confirms that graves of the Bourbons are in the Armenian cemetery in Agra. The tombs in the photographs appear to be those of descendants of John Philippe Bourbon of Navarre. Grave number 162 is that of Annie Bourbon (Simi Bibi), daughter of Inayat Masih, and wife of Pedro Bourbon. Number 163 is that of Pedro Bourbon, alias Imdad Masih, son of Captain Khairat Masih. Pedro Bourbon died in Bhopal. (Please see the Bourbon family tree for more details.) Father Joseph Tieffenthaller provided maps of the tombs of the Bourbons residing at the Bourbon Colony at Narwar, during his service at Narwar as a priest between 1747 and 1765 (Kochar 1994). Other graves are those of Christians massacred in Delhi and Narwar. More information on the Bourbons of Narwar is provided in the following chapter.

Tombs of Narwar
Source: Author's private collection

THE BOURBONS OF SHERGARH AND NARWAR

The story of Shergarh began with Akbar giving the town as a gift to Jean Philippe de Bourbon for serving in his army. After Jean Philippe, his sons took over Shergarh, which is not far from Narwar, in present day Madhya Pradesh. When Nadir Shah invaded Delhi in 1739, five generations of Bourbon descendants had served the Mughals. Francis Bourbon, the last man in charge of the imperial seraglio, narrowly escaped with his family. They took refuge in 'the Fort of Sirgarh' with 300 men and women (Saksena 1941, 197).

Shergarh or Sirghur (25° 35' North, 77° 58' East) was held as a Bourbon *jagir* in the territory of the Narwar chief. Akbar had given the title of 'Raja,' or king of Shergarh, to Jean Philippe de Bourbon. The Bourbons were rich and powerful, but this title came with a great sense of honour and responsibility. Mesrovb Seth writes, 'In the year 1742, a rich Christian, who is held in great esteem by the King of the palace, built a new chapel for the gathered Christians' (Seth 1937,

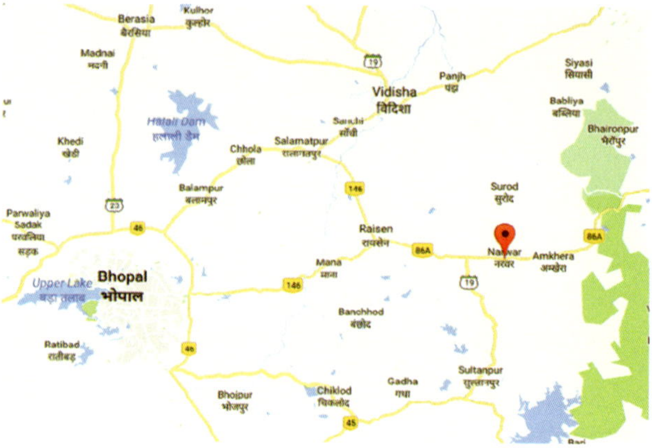

Map showing location of Narwar and Shergarh
Source: Google Maps

142). The Bourbons were given the Maratha fort of Shergarh to make their home near Narwar[1] in safety until 1778. Their lives resumed at Shergarh, where Francis Bourbon had three sons, Francis II, Saville, Salvador and a daughter Fakhr-un-Nisa.

According to Father A. Strobl, a Christian mission station and church, with a resident priest, was established in Narwar in 1743 (Seth 1937, 95). Strobl, who was there between the years 1743–1765, also wrote detailed accounts of the church and the Bourbon family.

Narwar Fort is situated atop a hill about 500 feet above ground level spread over an area of 8 sq. km that stands on a steep scarp of the Vindhya Range. It is now in a dilapidated condition, but the remains suggest that in its flourishing days, it might have been only second to the Gwalior Fort in magnificence. The interiors of the fort are divided by cross walls into four '*ahata*' and '*dholaahata*'. *Ahata* is a compound or a yard wall and *dholaahata* means two walls usually separating compounds or yards for men and women.

The architecture of the fort and palaces is essentially Rajput in style, with fluted columns, and a flat ceiling supported by many arches. The inner walls of the palaces have been decorated with bright paint and glass beads. Near the fort are the monuments such as the Jai Stambha, Sati monument, Ladu bungalow, Chhip Mahal, Makardwaj Tal, Kacheri Mahal, Sikandar Lodi's Mosque, and Jail Kambha. Traditionally said to have been the capital of Raja Nala, of the Sanskrit epic *Mahabharata,* the town was called Nalapura until the 12th century. After that time, Kachwaha, Parihar, and Tomar Rajputs (warrior communities) successfully held Narwar till the Mughals captured it in the 16th century.

According to *The Archaeological Survey of India Report Vol. 2,* Narwar was an important town and seat of a governor during the Mughal supremacy. It also included a Roman Catholic chapel as well as a burial ground with a walled cemetery. The enclosure was '115 feet by 83 feet, containing an entrance room, a small chapel, and 50 tombs.' The chapel was a small room, 21½ feet by 10½ feet. At the altar the letters I. H. S. were inscribed, surmounted by a cross. Of the tombs, only two bear inscriptions; one in Portuguese, the other in Persian (ASI 1871, 322).

Inscriptions at Narwar, dated 1743, mark the resting place of an Armenian military officer and honour the memory of an Armenian priest at Narwar. These are proof of the existence of a family and a larger Armenian community in Narwar during the mid-18th century. Records and maps drawn by two previously mentioned Catholic priests, Father

A. Strobl and Father Tieffentaller, who lived at Narwar during that period, also confirm the presence of a Christian community. Both priests are also buried in Narwar.

Ruins of Shergarh Fort
Source: Author's private collection

In *Christianity in Asia and America, after A.D. 1500*, by John Francis Butler, Father Antonio Montserrat (1536–1600) states, 'Throughout, the Mission made great use of art, but primarily of architecture as at Goa. Churches were built in the large Court Towns, a chapel at Narwar.' (Butler 1979, 8). Michael Fisher, in the *Visions of Mughal India: An Anthology of European Travel Writing* notes that the Fathers were astonished to see 13 statues of half-length carved in the wall of the vestibule of one of the temples. Judging by the style and the position, the middle statue appears to represent Christ, with six statues to his right and six to his left, who appear to represent the Apostles. Three hundred years ago, Christians inhabited this district, but over the years they were defeated by Muslims, who effectively cleared all signs of Christianity in the region. This history of battle is why Narwar was embellished with a strong fortress on the top of the hill.

According to Colonel Kincaid, Francis Bourbon, great-grandson of Jean Philippe de Bourbon, came to Narwar with his entire clan of around 300 relatives and family who settled in Narwar shortly after the plunder of Delhi in 1739 (Kincaid 1887). Three miles

Ruins of the fort at Shergarh
Source: Author's private collection

from there lay the ruins of the Fort of Shergarh, which had been entrusted to Francis. Father Tieffentaller was stationed at Narwar between July 1747 and the beginning of 1750 and again between December 1751 and 1765, as the chaplain of the Bourbon family. He writes that after the Raja's palace, one of the finest buildings within Narwar Fort was the palace of a certain Christian born of Armenian parents, admitted to the government of a Hindu Raja of the province, and loaded with honours and favours by the Mughal Emperors. He had houses built for all his family, and a chapel to pray in. On feasts and Sundays, a Jesuit father held mass at the chapel, where a large community of Christians used to gather. Kincaid corroborates that Francis de Bourbon was born in 1680 and married an Armenian lady, 'a relative of his own' in 1710 (Kincaid 1887, 166).

The foundation of the church at this little town in Central India forms an interesting feature of the work of the missionaries. The Narwar Ruler of the

State was a Hindu, but after Nadir Shah ransacked Delhi, a Christian person of some importance obtained considerable influence in his durbar. The Jesuit letters are somewhat mysterious regarding the identity of this person, but tradition speaks of him as one of the family of Indian Bourbons. Under his auspices, a church was built, and the Raja funded the maintenance of a resident priest and provided for the poorer Christians. The Jesuits stationed a missionary at Narwar from about 1742, and the congregation consisted of the relatives of the Christian nobleman. These congregants were of low position, but they were sufficiently well-off to afford from time to time a contribution for the needs of their still poorer fellows, the Christians in Agra. This small congregation gradually dwindled away and, in 1765, the priest in charge, being apparently no longer supported by the State, found it necessary to abandon his station. By the mid-18th century, there are records of five churches at Mogor (Mughal) proper: one at Narwar, one at Jaipur, one at Agra, and two at Delhi.

Ruins at Shergarh
Source: Author's private collection

During 1946, my family was based at Gwalior. My father, Colonel S. C. Ghosal, was the General Manager of Gwalior & North India Transport (G.N.I.T), owned by Maharaj Jivajirao Scindia. Narwar was not very far from Gwalior, and we planned a family trip. My mother, Magdaline Bourbon, was very keen to see the Narwar ruins and narrated a story that she heard from her grandmother, Veronica Bourbon, wife of Bonaventura Bourbon, about the Narwar massacre. The massacre wiped out the entire colony, including the Armenians and the clergy; only Salvador II, his mother, and three children could leave Shergarh. Recent excavation of the big tank at Narwar showed a Roman Catholic chapel and some tombs that resemble a Christian burial ground. Another unique discovery was an iron gun of Sawai Jai Singh of Amber (according to the State Archives of Madhya Pradesh). If excavations continue, ruins linked to the Bourbon family might be brought to light.

The only excavated structure that can be attributed to Hindu rule is a large tank called Magar-Dhwaj [or Makara Dhwaja]. The name is Hindu and said to be a link to the Raja under whose expense it was excavated. The work must have been rather costly, as the tank is 300 square feet at the top and 35 to 36 feet deep, and carved from one solid rock. The tank is now dry, except during the rainy season.

Ruins of fort at Shergarh
Source: Author's private collection

In 1779, the Raja of Narwar, who was jealous of Francis Bourbon, his feudatory, attacked Shergarh. Rousselet (1975) notes that the Bourbons were dethroned by a French adventurer named Captain Fantome, who worked for the Scindia family of Gwalior. Along with almost every member of his family, Salvador Bourbon was massacred in the attack at Narwar. Salvador Bourbon alias Ghulam Masih's son also known as Salvador Bourbon (Inayat Masih, born in 1760, age 18), and his cousin, Pedro Bourbon, survived the attack. Salvador fled Narwar with his mother, whose maiden name was Bervette, and two or three younger Bourbon children (Kincaid 1887, 167). They reached Gwalior, where they were helped by the local Christian families. Salvador Bourbon was appointed *Qiledar* (commander) of Gwalior Fort (Malcolm 1832; Saksena 1941).

In 1780, Maratha Mahadji Scindia captured Gwalior Fort. Later that year, an Englishman named Colonel Popham, of the East India Company, captured the fort. Sir John Malcolm explains that Salvador Bourbon met Colonel Comac, who sympathized with him and gave him some money, a good house, and a village in Ichhawar *tehsil* (Malcolm 1823, 421). Ichhawar is a town in the Nizamat-i-Maghrib (Western District) of Bhopal state, Central India, located at 23° 2' North, 77° 1' East. The site is an old one, the present town having been built on the foundations of the village of Lakshmipura. A small fort had been built by the Marathas, who had earlier seized it in 1716.

The Ichhawar *tehsil* was held in *jagir* for many years by the Bhopal Bourbons, as a reward for their loyalty to the Bhopal State and many valiant episodes involving saving the life and throne of the Begums of Bhopal.[2] The two villages granted by the *Sanad* in Gwalior were Barnai and Sikrai. After Salvador settled the family, his mother, Bervette, advised him to go to Bhopal and seek help under the wives of Nawab Yar Mohammad Khan. Salvador followed his mother's advice and, with his cousin Pedro, went to Bhopal in 1785.

Endnotes

1. Narwar was said to be in a town and district in Agra, south of the Chambal River, near Chittore (24° 2′ North, 75° East). Narwar was subsequently under the rule of the Scindia family (Malcolm 1824).

2. Ichhawar was later given over to Bhopal State under the Treaty of 1818.

THE BOURBONS OF BHOPAL

When Yar Mohammad Khan, the Nawab of Bhopal, died in 1742, he left behind Mamola Bai and another wife, Asmat Begum, as well as his children by the latter. Mamola Bai (1715–1795) was childless, but took care of Faiz Mohammad Khan and the other sons of Asmat Begum so lovingly that they called her Manji. Manji Mamola became de facto ruler of Bhopal. Sometimes recognized as the first woman ruler of Bhopal, she ruled the state for 50 years.

In her later years, Manji Mamola fell ill. Legend has it that Shah Ali Shah, a saint, heard this news and, believing that Mamola Bai could do much more good for the people of Bhopal than he could, decided to give 10 years of his life to her. He is said to have taken a bath and put on a *Kafan* (a dress Muslims wear when buried). Soon after he passed away. Manji Mamola recovered and died about 10 years after this incident. The saint's dargah or burial ground is known as Shah Ali Shah's Takia in Bhopal's Big Lake or *Bada Talab*. Due to an increase in water levels after the creation of

Bhadbhada Dam, water surrounded this place and it is now an island. Many devotees visit this dargah and in the summer, sometimes, water levels decrease, making it easier for people to walk to this sacred place and offer prayers.

Shrine of Shah Ali Shah in the middle of the *Bada Talab* (Big Lake)
Source: Author's private collection

At the time Salvador Bourbon came to Manji Mamola, in 1785, Bhopal needed allies to counter the British forces. Mamola Bai had a keen political and administrative acumen. She realized the fast-growing influence of the British and was the first to offer a hand of friendship to Salvador. Much like the Scindias bestowing upon Jean Baptiste Filose, also a Frenchman, the position of General in the army of Gwalior, Mamola Bai offered Salvador the position of General in the Bhopal State army, as well as gifted him land to ensure that he would reside in Bhopal State. In addition, she also bestowed upon Salvador a Muslim name, Inayat Masih, to pacify the orthodox Pathans and suggested that Salvador would adopt Muslim ways of living in Bhopal. Thus, Salvador took service under Manji Mamola. In 1786, Salvador married Miss Thome. Slowly adapting to the Bhopali style of living, Salvador and his cousin Pedro gave up their way of dressing and started wearing Bhopali garb, though they did not convert to Islam. They eventually became the leading figures of the Bhopal court (Kincaid 1887, 164–77). Pedro, who had been given the Muslim name Imdad Masih, continued to live in Icchawar and died in 1833, leaving behind his son Anthony (also named Khairat Masih, born in 1734). Pedro's wife was known as Madam

Bourbon. Khairat Masih was married to Louisa Bourbon (maiden name Frances) and appointed as Commander of the Cavalry of Bhopal. Like other Bourbons, he served the Bhopal State with much loyalty, particularly when confronted with mutiny.

Salvador Bourbon
Source: Author's private collection

During his time at the Bhopal court, a Hindu lady and her son sought the help of Salvador Bourbon. She had been a mistress of Diwan Chote Khan. Salvador Bourbon was not only a brilliant strategist, and a highly educated man with a good family history, but also an honourable man with a kind heart. He adopted the lady's son as his own to save the lady from being killed by Chote Khan. This boy was called Bertram when he was young and later on was called Balthazar. Ram Babu Saksena also confirms that there is uncertainty about Balthazar's real name as the name Bertram appears in the writings from time to time. National Archival documentation (Sanad and Jagir file no 514/1 Inayat Masih National Archives) also confirms that Balthazar Bourbon was the son of a previous mistress of Diwan Chote Khan. Manji Mamola Bai trusted Salvador Bourbon. He remained in her services as *Tehsildar* and *Thanedar* until her death in 1795.

After the death of Manji Mamola, Diwan Chote Khan had a quarrel with Salvador and managed to kill his former mistress. Salvador had to leave Bhopal with her son Bertram, whom he adopted as Balthazar Bourbon or Shahzad Masih. Chote Khan died in 1795, and Wazir Mohammad Khan became the official ruler of Bhopal, even though he never assumed the title of Nawab. Wazir Mohammad Khan invited Salvador back to Bhopal to become Commander-in-Chief. In 1796, Salvador Bourbon (Inayat Masih) thus returned to Bhopal with his family. The father and son alliance of Wazir Mohammad Khan and his son Nazar Mohammad Khan with Inayat Masih and his son Balthazar Bourbon won many battles together. Their joint trials in a context of external adversity highlighted the character and loyalty of the Bourbons and strengthened a steady friendship between the Bourbons and the Nawabs and Begums of Bhopal.

In 1800, Salvador had been granted a *jagir* of two villages. Two descendants of the Bourbon family, Balthazar Bourbon and thereafter his son Sebastian Bourbon, became Prime Ministers to the Begums of Bhopal. The fleur-de-lis is part of the royal coat of arms of the Bhopal royal family, as a tribute to the service of this branch of the Bourbon family. The Bourbons were said to be the most influential family in Bhopal and were counted as one of the wealthiest families in the city (Kincaid 1887, 164–77).

Extreme left: Fleur-de-lis
Source: Wikimedia Commons (Public domain) https://commons.wikimedia.org/wiki/File:Fleur_de_lys_(or).svg

Left: Bhopal State Coat of Arms with the Fleur-de-lis
Source: Wikimedia Commons (Public domain) https://commons.wikimedia.org/wiki/File:Bhopal_State_CoA.png

Wazir Mohammad Khan, Salvador Bourbon, and the Bhopal seige of 1812

In one of their most memorable victories, Balthazar Bourbon and his father Salvador played a major role in the 1812 Siege of Bhopal. Nazar Mohammad Khan closed all the gates of Bhopal, including Fategarh Fort, for nine months, to secure the city from a Maratha army coalition of Nagpur and Gwalior. The British East India Company refused to help Bhopal, as they did not trust the Wazir. Salvador was aware that the Marathas outnumbered the Bhopalis and defeat was imminent. The Bhopal army of about 2,500 men comprised around 600 Pathans along with Sheikhs, Syeds, and Sikhs and were outnumbered by the 80,000 Marathas. With the Bhopal city gates closed, there was no food for the residents. Bathazar jumped into the lake multiple times with a *mushuk*s (leather bag) to bring food for the people. He swam across the lake to bring food and water from some faithful Rajput *zamidar*s (landlords). According to my mother, Magdaline Bourbon, Hindus and Christians fought side by side with Nazar Mohammad Khan to save Bhopal.

In this tense time of war, Bhopali women played a very important role. Zeenat Begum, wife of Ghous Mohammad Khan (5th Nawab of Bhopal, 1807), led Hindu and Muslim women to fight against the Marathas. These women came out in full force, helped throw boiling water on the enemy, and even prepared bombs. They also helped fill gunpowder in the shells and fire cannons. The women's brigade was responsible for the supply of food and water. Women wore men's battle armour and stood on the wall of the fort to show the Marathas that they had enough manpower to fight. Surprisingly, the enemies withdrew and Bhopal was saved. Wazir Mohammad Khan praised the role of women and their bravery. My mother often used to say that there is something in the water of Bhopal Lake that makes women very brave. Even today, Bhopali ladies simultaneously lead traditional and non-traditional lives. They wear churidar pyjamas and loose kurtas, with long dupattas, which comprise the traditional dress of Bhopal. They play an active role outside the home driving jeeps as well as looking after their husbands and families.

Having been previously repelled by Salvador Bourbon and Wazir Mohammad Khan, the Marathas again joined together to re-attack Bhopal in March 1812, at the time of Dussehra. Jagua Bapu, Scindia's general from Gwalior, and Sadiq Ali from Nagpur hatched a plan for the total annihilation of Bhopal. They agreed that the Bhopal territory would be equally split between their two armies. When Wazir Mohammad Khan became aware of this plot he asked all the inhabitants to leave Bhopal to avoid the risk of yet another pending siege. Many Bhopalis followed orders and left the city. This siege began in September 1812 and lasted four months. Jagua Bapu brought 25,000 men, Dan Singh had 12 battalions of 12,000 men and 30 guns, Ram Lala and Krishna Bhao brought 15,000 men, and Sadiq Ali of Nagpur brought 30,000 men. Bhopal had only a force of 11,000 men. This number included state troops numbering 6,000, as well as 3,000 men under Namdar Khan Pindara, and 2,000 men associated with Ratan Singh Thakur of Satunbari and zamindars of the Tal Pargana.

During the first fortnight, the fighting consisted of firing of cannons from both sides. After 15 days, taking permission from Wazir Mohammad Khan, Namdar Khan left with most of the mounted troops of the zamindars. They all promised support in the provision of much-needed grains. They fulfilled their promise and kept sending grains from the side of the old fort. Sadiq Ali of Nagpur found out about this route and immediately blocked the road to Ginnori Gate. Ram Lala and Krishna Bhao also blocked other gates. The number of forces within Bhopal stood at a reduced number of only about 3,100. This was the real test for Wazir Mohammad Khan. Wazir and Salvador came up with a plan of attack. They asked for the following deployment of soldiers: The old fort under Dunger Singh with 100 men; Jai Singh at Ginnori Gate with 200 men; Syed Baqar Ali at Budhwara Gate with 200 men; Syed Barashna Nanga Sir (bare head, as he never covered his head) with 200 men at Mangalwara Gate; Mulaim Khan with 200 men at Itwara Gate; Khwaja Baksh Chela at Jumerati Gate with 200 men; Nawab Muiz Mohammad Khan, son of Ghous Mohammad Khan, with 400 men at Peer Gate; Karam Mohammad Khan with 200 men at Imami Gate; Lala Gulshan Rai with 500 men at Wazir Ganj (or Bis Hazari Khirki) suburb; Dil Mohammad Khan with 400 men at Fateh Garh Fort; 100 men inside the Fort of Bala Qila with Zalim Singh; and 100 men at Fateh Garh

Gate with Shuja Khan. Wazir Mohammad Khan and Salvador Bourbon kept 500 men with them to patrol the city.

The enemy fired around 40 guns every day, more during phases of attack. Wazir Mohammad Khan gave strict orders not to fire unnecessarily. Boats brought grains across the upper lake until even this scanty supply of food was blocked when the enemy bribed the boatmen. In the middle of December, a general assault took place. A storming party was directed on every gate, while others tried to climb the walls. They were taken down on every point, though the onslaught continued for 18 hours. Wazir Mohammad Khan and Salvador Bourbon continuously checked each gate, which gave great courage and confidence to the troops and inhabitants.

In January, Dan Singh assaulted Mangalwara Gate and Itwara ramparts and Sadiq Ali assaulted Ginnori Gate. At Mangalwara Gate the assailants ascended the walls, but the defenders repulsed them with support from Wazir Mohammad Khan, who chased the enemy from Itwara to Mangalwara Gate. They finally retreated. With this partial success, many gathered at Mangalwara Gate, and the defence of Ginnori Gate was neglected. The army of Nagpur put up ladders to enter Bhopal. Wazir Mohammad Khan immediately sent Salvador around the wall, where his men surprised the enemy with heavy artillery from behind. After about an hour's struggle, the enemies were forced to retreat and the ladders were brought down. In February Dan Singh made repeated attacks without success.

Jagua Bapu attacked on the north face of the wall and managed to knock it down in several places. The wall at Atta Shuja Khan was also knocked down and the enemy started to enter the city but Pathan women faced them with bricks and stones. Bahadur Mohammad Khan reached there with a few men and started to defend bravely. The enemy was about 5,000 men strong, but Bahadur Mohammad Khan, son of Mohammad Khan, continued to fight. Wazir Mohammad Khan soon reached there and provided assistance, as he was wounded. Wazir Mohammad Khan promised Bahadur one-fourth of his inheritance. Bahadur remained with Wazir in all his early fights.

During the same year, in February, Ram Lala decided to attack with 3,000 men. He marched by daybreak. The troops stationed at Fatehgarh Fort in Bhopal were alert and started to fire. Wazir Mohammad Khan found that two battalions of the enemy had entered Wazir Ganj, a suburb of Bhopal founded by Wazir. He fired two guns, killing 300 men on the spot. Meanwhile, Ram Lala continued to push at Fateh Garh. Wazir Mohammad Khan attacked with his men. In this battle the casualty rate was very high. Finally, the enemy had to retreat with their numbers reduced from 3,000 to just over 500 hundred.

Muiz Mohammad Khan, son of Ghous Mohammad Khan, was in charge of the defences at Peer Gate and Imami Gate, which were in the *jagir* of Muiz. On one occasion, there was too much pressure as Jagua Bapu directed his whole army on Peer Gate. Wazir Mohammad Khan attacked them with his reserve army, who were hiding in the ruins. But Wazir got surrounded by the troops of Diwan Gulshan Rai. There was chaos in the area, and after a fierce battle the enemy fled.

Wazir Mohammad Khan got the news that Mir Mohammad Aqil Khan was ascending the bastion of Atta Shuja Khan. There was a rumor that Mir Mohammad sent Wazir a message saying, 'By tomorrow where will you be and where I will be'. Hearing this, Wazir got suspicious and ascended the bastion with mustard seeds in a dish. He observed that the mustard seeds moved, so he immediately ordered his men to evacuate the bastion, as there was some digging going on. The next day, when the forces of Jagua Bapu arrived near Chota Talab, a lake near the bastion, the forces of Bhopal suddenly came out of the bastion and attacked Jagua Bapu's forces. Many were killed and the enemies withdrew. At the same time, Amir Mohammad Khan, son of Wazir Mohammad Khan, sent Aman Singh, a Patel of Rehti, with 200 bullock carts laden with wheat. Amir Mohammad Khan also encouraged Nathu Pindara to muster 500 horses to carry grain to the old fort by cover of night. However, Sadiq Ali Khan's men stopped him. In March, Jagua Bapu—in disgust—swallowed a diamond, committing suicide. His followers burnt his body in Islam Nagar and went back to Gwalior.

At the end of April, Dunger Singh was stationed at the old fort with only 10 men. He deserted his post at night, and 500 of the enemy entered the old fort. Two men stationed near the old fort got suspicious, hearing the bustle of Nagpur troops. They silently entered the old fort and discovered the enemy troops. They informed Wazir Mohammad Khan, who inquired about Dunger Singh, but the informers did not know anything about him. Dunger Singh's treachery was obvious to Wazir; he had allowed 500 enemies to enter the old fort and thus compromised the tomb of Nawab Faiz Mohammad Khan. Wazir Mohammad Khan asked his son, Nazar Mohammad Khan, to attack immediately.

Nazar Mohammad Khan, along with Salvador Bourbon, Syed Husain, Pirzada, Bakshi Bahadur Mohammad Khan, Mirza Kamal Beg, and Ghulam Muhi Uddin Ansari, immediately went to the old fort with only 12 men. Wazir Mohammad Khan followed at a short distance. The enemy was careless and, taking advantage of the situation, the Bhopal forces attacked them with guns, killing many on the spot. Wazir Mohammad Khan joined the party and, with a great show of bravery, pushed the enemy out. About 100 enemy men were killed and many were injured; the rest fled, leaving behind their arms. Thrown stones seriously bruised Wazir Mohammad Khan, and Nazar Mohammad Khan received a severe cut to his shoulder and a small cut to the head. Qazi Ameer Muhi Uddin Ansari, son of Qazi Ghulam Muhi Uddin Ansari, died in the battle with Bhao Rao's troops.

On one occasion, there was no gunpowder left, and the guns were silent. Wazir Mohammad Khan sent Maulvi Nizam Uddin and Qazi Mohammad Yusuf to establish a treaty with Sadiq Ali Khan asking him to retreat to Raisen. That very same night, Nathu

Pindara arrived with 300 hundred bullocks laden with gunpowder and 200 bullocks with grain, sugar and tobacco. Equipped with these new supplies, Wazir Mohammad Khan again started to fire at the enemy. His messengers came back angrily, because their message of peace had been accompanied with rounds of fire from the Bhopal forces.

Wazir Mohammad Khan was disheartened from the long siege and went to a religious saint named Mastan Shah. Wazir put his sword on his feet and said 'I have done what I could, now it's up to you'. Mastan Shah replied, 'You must keep fighting and the favour of God is with you again'. On this same day, Wazir Mohammad Khan and Nawab Ghous Mohammad Khan were surrounded by 10,000 men and 5,000 horses. Wazir Mohammad Khan and his men fought bravely. Syed Khair Uddin lowered ladders for them to climb the wall, even as his men kept firing from the cannon for protection. Wazir Mohammad Khan ordered Iqbal Khan to set fire to the city ruins so the enemy could not hide.

The next day, an elderly man approached Wazir Mohammad Khan and said his father had worked closely with Yar Mohammad Khan. He remembered his father telling him about a treasure hidden under one of the bastions. Wazir asked his forces to dig up the bastion and found 500 bags of gunpowder hidden in the basement of the fort, as well as 22 large sacks, each containing 8,000–10,000 pieces of copper and 30 small iron guns, in good condition. He directed the guns to be mounted on the walls, while the copper was coined and distributed to the troops.

This brought new life to the soldiers, who were disheartened and exhausted after many months of the siege.

The enemy, too, had enough of this prolonged siege and the unavailability of grain and grass for their horses. Sadiq Ali Khan retired, publicly announcing that he had a dream telling him not to attack Bhopal because the city was under the protection of divine providence. Dan Singh and other commanders tried to persuade Sadiq Ali to continue with the seige, but he replied, 'You should follow the same if you wish to avoid the heavens' vengeance'. After a fortnight, the others followed suit, stopped the siege, and moved towards Sarangpur.

Hearing the news of the end of the siege of Bhopal, the Maharaja of Gwalior, Scindia got furious. He has suffered tremendous losses during the siege. He again sent his forces under the famous general John Baptiste Filose. The forces came to Sehore, 23 miles from Bhopal. In March 1814, Scindia's generals, Jean Baptiste Filose (half-brother of Colonel Filose, who betrayed Nana Phadnavis) and Jaswant Bhao Rao (son of Jewa Dada, the brother of Jagua Bapu), attacked Bhopal and again besieged the city. Jean Baptiste brought with him a well-equipped brigade of eight battalions and about 40 guns. This was a critical time for Bhopal because resources were already on the lowest ebb. Even the Pindaris joined the Scindias. Not much ammunition was left in Bhopal. The siege continued for six months. There was no food in the town, so the Muslim women ate *chalia* (beetle nut) and cooked leather goods while

Hindu women ate bishop's weed and the seeds and bark of tamarind trees. They even used stones, warm water, oil, and half burned ash to defend their town. Most of the walls of the city were in bad shape, so it was not easy to defend.

Wazir Mohammad Khan knew that this time it would be impossible to fight the Gwalior forces. He sent Salvador Bourbon to meet the invading General, as he needed time to approach the British to intervene. Salvador Bourbon and John Baptiste Filose met and followed the tradition of exchanging turbans. Filose at once said, 'We are both sons of France, why should we fight?' (Boulger 1887, 169). According to W. S. Davis, a political agent in Bhopal, 'Filoze's geography was at fault, no doubt, father having been a Neapolitan; but he had been born and brought up among Scindia's French battalions, and probably his sympathies were with the French.' The British referred to him as 'that confounded fellow, John the Baptist.' Thus, the British intervened and Bhopal was saved. The Bourbons of Bhopal were very proud of this exchange, as it felt like a miracle and saved Bhopal from being defeated. Doulat Rao Scindia's generals, Jean Baptiste Filose and Jaswant Bhao Rao, fell out and started to fight between themselves at Sehore. Jean Baptiste is said to have taken with him 103 guns of different sizes, so the followers of Jaswant Rao fled and took refuge in Bhopal for a short time. They were requested to depart the next day and, due to further political developments, Scindia ordered his army to withdraw. At the same time, Sadiq Ali was also ordered to withdraw by Nagpur's Chief.

After this second attack of Marathas and Pindaris in 1814, Wazir Mohammad Khan again sent Salvador to Nagpur on a peace mission. Accompanying Salvador were Karam Mohammad Khan and Mohammad Din Khan. Salvador had multiple rounds of correspondence with political agents such as Mr Carnac, General Brown, W. Jenkins, and Lord Minto. Salvador agreed to many terms proposed by the British agent Mr Wanchoupe, except the handing over of a fort. He was successful in his negotiations. In January 1815, Salvador wrote to a British agent that he would conclude this treaty after Muharram (the Muslim festival). After arrival back in Bhopal from Nagpur, Salvador died in December 1815. Balthazar Bourbon, Salvador's son, succeeded him. Salvador also left behind a daughter, Pascola, who received a sum of Rs. 1,500 per annum for her maintenance. Shortly before Salvador's death, Wazir Mohammad Khan had sanctioned the grant of a landed property of Rs.12,000 per year for his great service to the Bhopal state; however Salvador did not live to enjoy this hard-earned reward.

On an expedition in 1816, Wazir Mohammad Khan fell ill in Timaroun village. He tried to reach Bhopal, but died in Deori on 16 Rabi ul Sani (16 March AD 1816) after a four-day fever. Some of his close friends say that he was addicted to liquor in his last days. He died at the age of 51 (52 in Hijra years). Hakim Shahzad Masih (Balthazar Bourbon) brought his corpse from Deori to Bhopal and he rests in peace in Bara Bagh Bhopal, his own garden. He was a real hero in the history of Bhopal; he repeatedly saved Bhopal in difficult times. He was, in fact, the real Nawab, but he never acquired that title. He left behind two sons, Amir Mohammad Khan, who was older, and Nazar Mohammad Khan.

Nazar Mohammad Khan and the Treaty with the Honourable East India Company

During his lifetime, Wazir Mohammad Khan had selected Nazar Mohammad Khan (born in 1791) as his heir and raised him to the position of Wazir of Bhopal. Though Ghous Mohammad Khan was the Nawab, he had long retired and his name was simply used as a seal. He had nothing to do with affairs of state. Ghous Mohammad Khan remained in Raisen, a small district close to Bhopal. Relations between the two families became normal mainly because of the heroism of Wazir Mohammad Khan during the siege on Bhopal and because Wazir and Nazar both gave respect to Nawab Ghous Mohammad Khan. Nazar was raised to the position of Minister and, in practice, to the position of Nawab. Nawab Ghous Mohammad Khan made no objection. His elder brother, Amir Mohammad Khan, publicly announced Nawab Ghous Mohammad Khan's non-ability to fulfill that role. Nazar Mohammad Khan consented and took the title Nazir-ud-Doula.

Nazar Mohammad Khan commissioned the Gauhar Mahal palace in 1815-16, and then married daughter of Nawab Ghous Mohammad Khan, Gauhar Begum, on Friday 22 Rabi ul Sani AH 1232 (28 February AD 1817), to strengthen the ties between the two

Nawab Nazar Mohammad Khan
Source: Author's private collection

families. Nazar Mohammad Khan and his new wife moved to Gauhar Mahal, and his minister and friend Balthazar Bourbon aka Shahzad Masih built a *haveli* (mansion) nearby. This haveli is now part of Shaukat Mahal palace.

Nazar Mohammad Khan, like his father, prioritized a treaty with the British government. He sent Shahzad Masih to Mr Jenkins in Nagpur on his behalf in early 1818. Mr Jenkins agreed to the same terms that he had agreed to with Wazir Mohammad Khan in 1814. Nazar sent Hakim Shahzad Masih as an envoy to Hoshangabad to render all possible support to General Adams. Nazar was offered the same terms and accepted without hesitation. Sir Thomas Hislop and Sir John Malcolm bargained the smaller details.

The treaty between the Honourable East India Company and the Nawab Nazar Mohammad Khan, Ruler of Bhopal, was concluded by Captain Josiah Stewart on the part of the Honourable Company, in virtue of full powers granted by His Excellency, The Marquis of Hastings, K.G. Governor General, etc. and by Khurram Mohammad Khan Bahadur and Shahzad Masih Sahib on the part of the Nawab Nazar Mohammad Khan in virtue of full powers granted by the Nawab in 1818. This treaty with 11 Articles was concluded at Raisen on 26 February 1818, and signed by J. Stewart (political agent), Khurram Mohammad Khan, and Shahzad Masih. Governor General Lord Hastings ratified the treaty on 8 March 1818 at Lucknow.

This treaty had three significant features. First, recognition of Nazar Mohammad Khan as a Nawab by the British. Second, the State of Bhopal had to furnish 600 horses and 400 infantrymen for the service of the British government and cede the fort of Nazargarh (Gulgaon). Third, the 'Panj Mahal', or five districts, taken from a *jagirdar* of Peshwa—Ashta, Ichawar, Sehore, Doraha and Devipura, and Islam Nagar (held by Scindia at the time)—were finally awarded to Nawab Nazar Mohammad Khan on 22 Zilhaj AH 1233 (3 October AD 1818). After completion of the treaty, a political agent was appointed. A place in Sehore was selected for this purpose. A cantonment with 1,000 men, including cavalry and infantry from the Bhopal Army, was placed under the political agent. Nawab Nazar Mohammad Khan, in order to make the payment required by the 1818 Raisen treaty, willingly sold his personal belongings and collected Rupees 51 lakhs. Even though the British always called Nazar Mohammad Khan 'Nawab', he never assumed that title due to his intimacy with Nawab Ghous Mohammad Khan. Muiz Mohammad Khan was not happy with this agreement, but, unable to do anything, he kept silent. During this time, many Bhopalis who had previously left to avoid the attacks came back to settle in the city, making houses of mud and tiles.

On 22 Muharram AH 1235 (11 November AD 1819), Nazar Mohammad Khan went to Islam Nagar to hunt, bringing with him his one-year-old daughter, Sikandar Jahan Begum, who had been born on 28 Shawwal AH 1233 (31 August AD 1818). Eight-year-old Foujdar Mohammad Khan, who was with Nazar and his daughter, took the pistol from the belt of Muiz Mohammad Khan (eldest son of

Nawab Ghous Mohammad Khan) and accidentally discharged it. The bullet went straight into Nazar Mohammad Khan's head. The British political agent Major Henley reported that, at the time of his death, Nazar Mohammad Khan had been playing with his daughter and had put his gun beside him. Foujdar Mohammad Khan, an 8-year-old was the only other person present. He was playing with a gun and accidentally shot Nazar. The bullet, after passing through Nazar's head, penetrated the wall of the mosque nearby.

Nazar Mohammad Khan was only 28 years old when he died. He had governed Bhopal for three years and five months. Balthazar Bourbon (Shahzad Masih) had been his Prime Minister. Malcolm states that Nazar had 'investigated every account himself, heard every complaint; and while all speak of his kindness, benevolence and justice, his memory is unstained by the reproach of a single act of tyranny.' Nazar left a will stating: 'Well wishers of the state, I hope the way you all supported me in management of the state, you will support my wife Qudsia Begum in ruling the state and when my daughter comes to age, she should be married to one of the relatives of the age and that her husband shall be the Ruler Nawab of Bhopal.'

Magdaline Bourbon and her Stories of Bhopal

My mother, Magdaline Bourbon, was a true Bhopali at heart. Even after her out-of-state marriage, she kept coming back to her roots in Bhopal. She used to speak of Bhopal in such nostalgic ways, particularly about the beautiful landscape. A favourite season in Bhopal is the monsoon, when the lakes swell and everything turns lush green. Bhopalis are very fond of water and they would all gather around when the Bhadbhada dam gates opended to drain excess rainwater. My mother used to talk about the good old days when Bhopali families would go out for picnics. She would narrate stories of Raja [King] Bhoj and Gangu teli, about an oil seller comparing himself with Raja Bhoj.

We also loved how my mother's expression used to change when she shared her favourite story of how Bhopal came to be. According to my mother, Raja Bhoj of the Paramara dynasty (1010–1055) founded Bhopal and ruled from his capital at Dhar. The name Bhoj-pal or Bhopal came about after the king's minister constructed a *pal* (dam). There is no archaeological evidence to support this claim, though a temple complex constructed by Raja Bhoj exists around 28 km from Bhopal.

Bhopal Dam built by Raja Bhoj
Source: Author's private collection

An alternative story claims that the name of the city was coined from the name of another king, who was called Bhupala. During his time, the first lake of Bhopal came into existence. There are three legends regarding the formation of the big lake that existed near Bhojpur. The first, as narrated by my mother, reflects the belief that the *Bada Talab* (big lake) is a (hu)man-made lake built by the orders of Raja Bhoj. But for many years, it did not have any water. Raja Bhoj was told that the pit would have water only if the first-born son and first-born daughter of two families were sacrified in the lake. One day, the marriage procession of a first-born son and daughter was passing by and the tragic couple met with an accident near the lake. Since then, the lake has never been empty. The second story is that Raja Bhoj had a mysterious disease, and to cure it he was told to bathe in water where 99 springs and 9 rivers meet. The third legend claims that when Raja Bhoj conquered some area to the south and wanted to distribute gifts to Brahmins, they refused to accept, saying they could not take these gifts from a sinner. Raja Bhoj was surprised to hear this and asked what sin he had committed. They replied that Raja Bhoj's mother had died because of him. When he was not yet born, astrologers told his father, Sandhupal, that it was not the right time for the birth of the baby boy but that if he *was* born, he would be a great king immediately. So, they hung his mother upside down until she died, after which the baby boy was born. The Brahmins told Raja Bhoj that, as penance, he had to perform a *yagna* (ritual prayer) and donate 99 gold coins, 99 silver coins, and 99 cows, to feed 99 Brahmins. The Raja was instructed to take a dip in water with 99 springs and 9 rivers, and then perform the *yagna*. Raja Bhoj decided to follow these instructions. When he constructed two dams near the Bhojpur temple, he was just two rivers short. At that time, a minister named Kalia told Raja

Chota Talab (Small lake), built by Diwan Chote Khan
Source: Author's private collection

Bhoj about the two rivers flowing through Bhopal, then called Kalia Srot. The area of the main lake was 250 square miles. Raja Bhoj decided to turn them towards Bhojpur by constructing a dam in Bhopal, thus bringing into existence the upper lake of Bhopal. Hoshang Shah later destroyed the main dam of Bhojpur. Bhopalis were always in praise of their lakes, *Bada Talab* (big lake) and *Chota Talab* (small lake), built by Diwan Chote Khan.

Tal hai to Bhopal Tal, baki sab talayyan,
Rani hai tho Kamlapati, baqi sab gadhayyan.

If there is a Lake, it is Bhopal Lake, all the others are mere ponds,
If there is a Queen, it has to be Kamlapati, all the others are mere mortals.

Endnotes

1. Though these *jagir*s were confiscated in 1817 during the reign of Nazar Mohammad Khan, one *moza* (village) dadar, Pargana Gulgaon (amounting to Rs 15,000), was restored in the year 1822 to Hakim Shahzad Masih and his brother Philip Bourbon, alias Imdad Masih.

BALTHAZAR BOURBON, ALIAS SHAHZAD MASIH

Balthazar Bourbon on his horse Mehboob
Source: Author's private collection

Balthazar Bourbon, alias Shahzad Masih, was a fascinating man of many qualities. He was a prolific writer and a linguist, well versed in Urdu, Farsi, and English. He was very well educated, though there are no records of his formal education. He was also a good administrator and a loyal servant of Bhopal State. A gallant and brave warrior, trusted by the rulers of Bhopal, Wazir Mohammad Khan and Nazar Mohammad Khan, Balthazar Bourbon was key to many successful battles, particularly during the famous siege of Bhopal in 1812. Both Balthazar and his father Salvador Bourbon were popular with the public. The Begums supported and respected the Bourbons, and on many occasions the Bourbons' loyalty to the Begums was tried and tested.

Tracing the trajectory of Balthazar's personal life and professional accolades has been difficult because there

are no proper records of his life history. It appears that in 1786 Salvador Bourbon II (1760–1815), who shared a name with his late father, married Miss Thome in Bhopal. Colonel William Kincaid notes that Balthazar was born in 1772, which may be inaccurate or implies that (a) Balthazar was born from an earlier marriage, or (b) Salvador was not Balthazar's biological father. However, the given birth year of Salvador II is 1760, which would make Salvador very young to have been married twice. Furthermore, given these dates, Balthazar was born when Salvador was only 12 years old, which is highly unlikely. Colonel Kincaid's document thus suggests that Balthazar did not actually belong to Salvador's bloodline.

Balthazar Bourbon smoking his hookah in Shaukat Mahal
Source: Author's private collection

Balthazar Bourbon with his bodyguards
Source: Author's private collection

In support of this conclusion, National Archival documentation shows that Balthazar Bourbon was born to Diwan Chote Khan's mistress, adopted by

Salvador II, and converted to Christianity. Ram Babu Saksena claims that Salvador had to leave Bhopal after the death of Manji Mamola in 1795, primarily due to a quarrel with Diwan Chote Khan. This quarrel had arisen because Diwan Chote Khan killed his former mistress, who was a Hindu lady and mother of his son.[1] The dates given specify that Salvador had come to Bhopal in 1785, when Balthazar was already 13 years old. Salvador then married Miss Thome in 1786 and they had three children: Philip,[2] Pascola, and Annie Bourbon.

In contrast, however, Sultan Jahan Begum, in *Tazkira-i-Baqi*, mentions that Balthazar was the eldest son of Salvador and Miss Thome, born in 1787, and that he died at the age of 42 in 1829. This document, then presents a counter-claim that Balthazar was born in 1787, and was the eldest son of Salvador and Miss Thome.

According to Ram Babu Saksena, there is also some uncertainty about Balthazar Bourbon's real name. The *Khum Khanai Jaweed* and the *European Shurai Urdu* mention his name as Balthazar, but the *Majmui Nagz of Qudrutullah Qasim*, which appears to be more reliable, gives his name as Bertram. Formal National Archival documents and previous research by various authors present different, often conflicting, details. Balthazar is often described in terms such as 'a son of a European, a friend and companion of Nawab Zafaryab Khan, son of Shamru, a pupil in poetry of Naseer', as well as a very brave man of great physical strength. According to Ram Babu Saksena, it was said that Balthazar could hold and keep a small elephant standing with his great strength and would not allow it to move (Saksena 1941, 219).

Nawab Sultan Jahan, Begum ruler of Bhopal, wrote in *Hayat-i-Qudsi* that Begum Qudsia, being young and in *purdah* (veil) after her husband Nazar Mohammad Khan's unexpected death, and given her responsibilies as mother of a toddler, could not dedicate much time for state administration. She decided to appoint four experienced people who would run the affairs of Bhopal State. At the top of this list was her husband's trusted friend, Balthazar Bourbon, described as '... descended from a Frenchman named Jean Philippe Bourbon, one of the interesting adventurers and believed to have been a member of the Royal Family of France who came to India in the reign of the Emperor Akbar' (Sultan Jahan Begum 1918, 24).

Balthazar Bourbon was a minister under Nawab Wazir Muhammad Khan. He acted as the Nawab's representative on many occasions, including his role as chief signatory of the Treaty of 1818. To obtain this important concession from the British government, Balthazar volunteered to bring a contingent of Bhopal troops to serve the British. To defray the cost, Wazir mortgaged his family's jewels. Balthazar, now well equipped with horses and troops, served the British with distinction, accompanying the British General Adams as far as Kotah. 'By this timely aid, Balthazar Bourbon won for the State, not only the long-sought-for treaty, but also five Purgunnahs and the Fort of Islamnugger (Kincaid 1887, 172).

This was not the only time Bourbons played a very important role as mediators between the rulers of Bhopal and the East India Company. Bhopal was a solitary Muslim state surrounded by the Hindu Maratha states of Gwalior, Indore, and Nagpur. These Hindu states were continually up in arms against Bhopal, often joining forces to attempt to take over Bhopal. At the same time, in-fighting between the royal families of Bhopal had also escalated. Salvador and Balthazar were both sent to negotiate between the East India Company and the royal family of Bhopal, and they succeded in their missions. The Bourbon name became so famous in the state that every foreigner who came to Bhopal in that era was known as Frances or Francesi.

Balthazar Bourbon's Service to Qudsia Begum and the Bhopal State

Wazir Muhammad Khan's death in 1816, which was soon followed by the death of his son, Nazar Mohammad Khan on 19 November 1819, deeply affected Balthazar Bourbon. Balthazar was very close to both men, and had spent years as their trusted political adviser. Just after Nazar Mohammad Khan's death, Karam Mohammad Khan, himself a state adviser like Balthazar, addressed a large public gathering that included the state army, members of the royal family, and other heads of state. Karam asked everyone to contemplate who should be the next ruler of Bhopal. Names of royal family members floated around, including Asaf Muhammad Khan, son-in-law and nephew of Nawab Wazir. But no decisions were taken right away. Balthazar said, 'I have no desire to have anything whatsoever to do with state affairs, but I will be responsible for three things, first, the management of the garden of the deceased, second, the palace which was his residence and whoever interferes with it will have to reckon with me, and lastly the pay of the army, and if any arrears are due I will be responsible for them and in fact am ready to pay them off now' (Sultan Jahan Begum 1918, 29).

Qudsia Begum, the first female ruler of Bhopal (1819 – 1837) Source: Author's private collection

To this, all replied: 'Whoever interferes with the Harem of the late Nawab is a man of no faith, but it is nevertheless necessary to arrange for the government of the State, so that the honour of the deceased ruler may be upheld and continue' (Sultan Jahan Begum 1918, 29).

Balthazar replied, 'This can be done if you accept Qudsia Begum as your ruler and obey her' (Sultan Jahan Begum 1918, 29).

Everyone accepted this proposal and it was agreed that the right of succession would go to Nazar's child, Sikandar Begum, as stipulated in Nazar Mohammad Khan's will. Since Sikandar Begum was very young at that time, Qudsia Begum was given the responsibility of state administration along with the assurance that to 'whomsoever she delegated her authority, he should be obeyed by all' (Sultan Jahan Begum 1918, 30). At this moment, Nawab Ghaus Muhammad Khan placed young Sikandar Begum in the arms of Balthazar Bourbon and said, 'carry out the duties of State and serve her as faithfully as you did the late Nawab' (Ibid., 31).

Balthazar was never enamoured with high positions, but he was very loyal, and thus promptly replied, 'This is impossible for me as all my ambition was centered in the Nawab and has died with him, Mian Karam Muhammad Khan must be her guardian' (Sultan Jahan Begum 1918, 29). This suggestion was not well received and, in the end, a compromise was sought. It was agreed that Karam Muhammad should supervise the state administration; Balthazar promised to assist him in the state affairs. This decision was communicated to Major Henley, the British political agent responsible for Bhopal State (Ibid.). Major Henley arrived in Bhopal a few days later. He asked Balthazar to accept the position of *diwan* (chief official). Again, Balthazar refused, saying that 'although he intended to lead a private life and abstain from being present at the Court, he would obey and assist Karam Muhammad Khan' (Ibid., 32). Finally, though, he did accept the position, and remained *diwan* until his death in 1829.

Upon the death of Nazar Mohammad Khan, it was Balthazar Bourbon, who became Qudsia Begum's trustworthy adviser. Nazar's mourning ceremony was attended by ambitious relatives who wanted to take the opportunity to rule Bhopal. As the prayer service ended, Qudsia Begum removed her veil and walked in the middle of the crowd to give a speech. Her speech was so powerful that nobody had the courage to stop her. Having been always in *purdah* until that moment, it was incredible that Qudsia Begum managed to find the courage to speak, with her face uncovered, in front of all the religious leaders and relatives. Shahjahan Begum in her work *The Táj-ul Ikbál Tárikh Bhopal* or *The History of Bhopal* mentions that within three days of her husband's death, Qudsia Begum proudly announced herself Regent. Mian Karam Muhammad Khan and Hakim Shahzad Masih, with the consent of Major Henley, the political agent in Bhopal, invested Qudsia Begum with the supreme authority of the State, while they continued to administer the state as her deputies (Shahjahan Begum, 1876).

When Qudsia Begum first became Regent, she did not participate in the administration of the state. It is mentioned in *Hayat-i-Qudsi* that her whole attention was towards her daughter. Her trusted men, including Hakim Shahzad Masih, Raja Kushwakht Rai, Mian Karam Mahommad Khan, and Bakshi Bahadur Mahommad Khan, handled her administration (Sultan Jahan Begum, 1918). Qudsia made Balthazar Bourbon a state administrator and gave him a *jagir* of Rs. 12,000 in the form of one village from his father Salvador's property and some cash.[3] Qudsia had on her side the common public and British political agents such as Major Henley, who was a staunch Bhopal State supporter. Major Henley asked Qudsia Begum to select a boy to be the future husband of Sikandar Begum. Amir Muhamad Khan, brother of Nawab Nazar Mohammad Khan, was the closest relative; his son Munir Muhammad Khan was selected. Balthazar Bourbon was sent to Amir Muhammad Khan with this proposal, though Qudsia Begum was not very happy with this selection. Amir agreed, but had the ulterior motive of making his son ruler of Bhopal, replacing Sikandar Begum.

Colonel Kincaid describes Qudsia Begum as a young girl of just 19 years surrounded by relatives seeking the throne. He further notes that if the relatives had an upper hand, it would have resulted in a civil war ending Bhopal State. It was only because of the guidance Qudsia Begum received from Balthazar Bourbon and a few others that Bhopal retained its prestige. Balthazar was a skilled administrator who was gifted another *jagir* of Rs. 34,000 per anum by Mr Maddock, agent to the Governor General in 1828.

An interesting view of the Begum is narrated by political agent Major Charters Macpherson, whose writing in 1854 suggests that all three Begums (Qudsia, Sikandar, and Shahjahan) were out of *purdah* (unveiled). The youngest of the three was then 16 years old. Major Macpherson elaborated that the Begums were unusual women in their times. The grandmother and mother rode horses, knew how to throw a spear, and were trained shooters. They were also capable of running the government and looking after their people. They had British tutors and spoke English with a European accent.

Major Macpherson further explained, 'I happened to say somewhat emphatically that everything depended on the way a system was worked, on the *umal* (action), that everything, in fact, was *umal*—and wished you had seen how she turned to her two ministers (Jamaluddin Khan and Lala Kishen Ram) and cried "Gentlemen, do you hear, that's for you. *Amal* is everything"' (*Gazetteer of India*, Bhopal State 1908, 32). Major Macpherson also added that the Begum showed 'fine Elizabethan taste in the choice of her officers of state' (Ibid.).

Qudsia Begum's reign marked the beginning of the great century of women's rule in Bhopal, where Qudsia ruled with strength from 1819 to 1837. She held *durbar* (great ceremonial gatherings), displayed military skills, learned to use weapons, and rode horses and elephants. Very unlike Muslim women of those times, she removed her veil. She was also successful in convincing British representatives that her rule was beneficial for the people of Bhopal. With the help of Balthazar Bourbon, she became a good diplomat and administrator. She had waterworks built and pipelines laid throughout Bhopal State, and established a water pumping station for the people of Bhopal.

However, the Pathans, especially the men, could not accept a woman's rule. They kept revolting, but with supporters like the Bourbons, the Begums continued to rule and develop Bhopal and look after the needs of the common people. Balthazar Bourbon played an important role; not only did he manage the State's administration, he was also accepted as part of the royal family, much as his father Salvador had been taken in by Manji Mamola.

Assassination plot against Balthazar Bourbon

As mentioned, the rule of the Begums was met with constant opposition. When Amir Khan's son was proposed as a suitable match for Begum Sikandar, who was still a young girl, he wrote to Major Henley. Amir stated in the letter that, after marriage, Munir would become ruler of Bhopal. Major Henley was a strong supporter of Qudsia Begum and reminded him of the agreement that Nawab Nazar Mohammad's daughter, Sikandar Begum, and her children had the rights to succession. Matters subsided, but Amir and his son, Munir, continued to create unrest during Qudsia Begum's reign. Amongst their revolts was a plot to assassinate Balthazar Bourbon. As narrated in *Hayat-i-Qudsi*, Amir planned an attack on Balthazar to kill him and seize the Begums soon after. This was planned for the day of the *tazia*[4] procession. Balthazar Bourbon used to accompany the *tazia* of Mir Ghulam Shah from the Shia sect of Muslims on the 10th day of Muharram. This *tazia* was constructed in Nazar Mohammad Khan's mausoleum and escorted by Sikandar Begum's cavalry. The plan was to cause a riot in the procession and murder Balthazar. Qudsia Begum and Balthazar received information of this plot. Qudsia sent Sikandar to Nawab Moiz Muhammad Khan for safety. She also asked Balthazar not to participate in the *tazia* procession. But Bathazar, being very brave, informed the Begum that nothing could scare

Muharram in Bhopal
Source: Author's private collection

him from participating in this yearly ritual. He gallantly rode on his famous horse, Mahboob, towards Munir Khan's party with a few mounted attendants, leaving the Begums behind. He ordered his attendants to beat Munir Khan's party with the 'butts of their lances' (Sultan Jahan Begum 1918, 37), rather than using their arms. *Hayat-i-Qudsi* states that the enemies were too 'contemptible' to use arms on. Since this move was unexpected, and Munir and his followers were stunned by Balthazar's bravery, they decided to disperse. It seems, though, that many died during the *tazia* procession; their graves and a mosque were constructed at the location in Karbala in 1835, labelled 'Masjid Ganj-i-Shaheedan' (mosque of the martyrs place). This mosque still exists in Bhopal.

Masjid Ganj-i-Shaheedan
Source: Author's private collection

This did not stop Munir from creating more trouble during Qudsia Begum's administration. He started to interfere in state affairs. Qudsia and Balthazar were both becoming very impatient with Munir's actions. This resulted in Mian Karam Muhammad Khan and Balthazar resigning from their positions, even though the Begum repeatedly requested them to revoke their resignations. Major Henley himself wrote asking Balthazar to reconsider his resignation. He noted that 'the Nawab (Munir Khan) was quite ignorant of the work of proper administration of the State, and that it was impossible to carry on the duties of a ruler without their help, if they left him to his own devices matters would go from bad to worse and blame would attach to them' (Sultan Jahan Begum 1918, 38). Balthazar agreed to continue his work as *Diwan*, which he did until his death in 1829.

Meanwhile, Major Henley and Qudsia Begum continued to threaten Munir Khan and asked him to stop his misconduct. This had no effect. Munir gained possession of the Raisen Fort through conspiracy and gathered his supporters. They planned to surround the houses of the Begum's supporters in Bhopal on order to ransack them and dishonour their women. Rumors of this conspiracy reached Balthazar. After his usual evening prayer, he summoned all officials to have a discussion to counteract Munir's plans. Bakshi Bahadur Muhammad, who was also present in the meeting, asked that the Bhopal gates be strongly guarded. Bakshi said he would attack Munir and his followers before they could reach Bhopal. He asked all the officials to assemble at Balthazar Bourbon's house and told Balthazar to be on guard in case his help was needed in the siege. A regiment of the army waited at Balthazar's residence awaiting the next move. Bakshi and his army won the five-day battle and recaptured Raisen Fort, though Bakshi himself did not survive the fight. Defeated, Munir relinquished all of his claims to be ruler of Bhopal State, and Sikandar Begum was given in marriage to Jahangir Muhammad Khan, Munir's younger brother.

Qudsia Begum relied on Balthazar Bourbon so much that there were rumours about them being lovers. But, according to my mother, Magdaline Bourbon, Qudsia and Balthazar treated each other like brother and sister. When the Scindias captured

Qudsia Begum, they kept her in Ichhawar. It was Balthazar who fought and brought her back. When they reached Bhopal, she gave him her *dupatta* (long scarf) and he gave her his *saffa* (head scarf), and they became symbolically brother and sister. From then on, it became Balthazar's duty to protect her from enemies. Balthazar always lived near her residence. Qudsia lived in Gauhar Mahal and Balthazar lived in a *haveli* or palace called Shaukat Mahal adjoining it.

Top: Gauhar Mahal, was built by Nawab Nazar Mohammad, for his wife Qudsia Begum, in Bhopal

Above: Inner view of Gauhar Mahal where Qudsia Begum held her audiences
Source: Author's private collection

Shaharyar Khan narrates that Shahzad Masih had unmatched loyalty to Qudsia Begum, and that this could be either interpreted as romance or 'extraordinary commitment as loyalty between subject and ruler' (Khan 2000, 246). Khan narrates that Qudsia asked Shahzad Masih to find a European bride, and that he duly obeyed and married an English lady in Delhi. She was later known as Dulhan Sahib. However, according to my mother, Balthazar received no such directive from Qudsia.

Qudsia Begum made Balthazar Bourbon her adviser, and conferred upon him a *jagir* of Rs. 12,000 in 1232 Fasli (1826 AD), which he refused. Nawab Qudsia Begum also awarded him a monthly payment for the upkeep and salary of servants, elephants, horse riders, and soldiers to guard his palace. The same year, Shahzad Masih was awarded the right to own a freehold land that could pass from generation to generation, as well as a district. In 1235 Fasli Ichhawar was awarded to him.[5] After his death, though, Ichhawar was confiscated. Balthazar's widow, Madam Dulhan Sahib, pleaded to the English Political Agent Lancelot Wilkinson. He wrote back saying that, because the Nawab Jahangir Muhammad Khan did not favour her, he could do nothing. After Nawab Jahangir Muhammad Khan Sahib's death in 1254 Fasli, Nawab Sikandar Begum helped the Bourbon family by writing that the property should be released and returned to Balthazar's widow, Dulhan Sahib.

Dulhan Sahib, widow of Balthazar Bourbon, in 1867 Source: Wikimedia Commons (Public domain). From 'Le Tour du Monde', 1873; after a photograph by Louis Rousselet. https://commons.wikimedia.org/wiki/File:Madame_Elizabeth_de_Bourbon_-_May_1867.jpg

Balthazar Bourbon and other European Urdu Poets of Bhopal

In those days, people from many countries settled in Bhopal due to its favourable climate, beautiful lakes, and greenery. They married Indian girls and learned the local Hindi and/or Urdu languages. The Begums encouraged this pattern by giving them *jagir*s and *mansab*s. The most famous of these foreigners was Balthazar Bourbon of the Bourbon family, who claimed descent from the royal family of France. Foreign gentlemen such as Pereira,[6] De Silva, Baptist, and Kirguzo were employed either in the state army or as administrators. Many of the foreigners were from Armenia, Portugal, Turkey, and Afghanistan. The majority were Christians who were well educated and came from families with social capital. They were interested in literature and tended to be good warriors; some were retired army officers. This foreign cohort had literary interests, and many knew Farsi and were fluent in Urdu or Farsi poetry.

Balthazar and other foreigners who made Bhopal their home—including Hakim Lewis Sahib, Hakim John Sahib, Hakim Frances Sahib, and Isaac Sahib (who was appointed Headmaster of the Prince of Wales School in Bhopal)—started a trend of poetry that portrayed their foreign lives and identities through Urdu or Farsi poetry. Balthazar used to write poetry under the pen name Wasif Shahzada. His collection of Urdu poetry (*Shaeri*) is under the name of *Fitrat*. Despite his powerful warrior image, Balthazar's poetry confirms that he was romantic at heart. Though his poems are about a lady he loved, it seems he could not directly reveal his love for her. Her name does not appear in any of his writing, but she was clearly the inspiration for and subject of most of his work. She was always in his thoughts. In one verse he writes, [literal translation from Urdu to English]: 'Let me live, don't worry me. Oh, my love, don't worry me to that extent, that I can't bear.' In translating Balthazar's Urdu poetry into English, some of the original essense is inevitably lost in translation. In some cases, however, the translation does allow for the appropriate meaning to come through. For example:

I saw the extent of my love, when she left the side of
my rival and came to my house.
If you have seen the face of that lady, you have seen
the full moon in the sky.

Due to his great command of Urdu and Farsi, Balthazar's verses sound very melodious and sweet. He compared his muse to the Almighty;

for him she was like the Lord above. Very little of his poetry could be retrieved because the bulk of the family's written records were given away or destroyed. He worked on coarse paper, and the quality of the paper deteriorated over the years. Most of his work could not be salvaged. In those days, hardly any house did not have a library, and Bhopal was famous for its State-supported *mushaira*s (formal gatherings where poets gather to perform their works). Consistent with its history of late night literary and musical entertainment, Bhopalis prefer to dine in the open, and to sit down on roadside benches (*patia*s) to discuss world politics, hear songs, or gossip late into the night. It is still common to find Bhopalis thus engaged at 2 am. For centuries, it has been regular entertainment throughout the region to listen to the poetic form of *ghazal*s and *qawwali* devotional music in the evening. Balthazar used to frequent *mushaira*s, which were well attended by high dignitaries. He was a regular participant, who was well respected and widely liked. It is perhaps unusual for a nobleman to recite Urdu and Farsi poetry at night and work as an effective prime minister during the day—but Balthazar Bourbon was exceptional in all respects.

My mother was the dear friend of an elder from this family lineage called Acche Sahib; his Christian name was Jean Baptiste. He was also called Jean Sahib *Jagirdar* (man who owns property). He was another master of Urdu and Farsi poetry, and authored a volume of poetry in each language. A compilation of the poetry of Bhopal's foreign writers was published in *The Influence of English*

Literature on Urdu Literature (1924).[7] My mother often said Acche Sahib was our relative, even though he belonged to the Baptist family. The Baptist family had long been in India, and had converted to Islam after living many years in Bhopal. Acche Sahib had two sons, Noman and Irfan. Irfan, the younger son, for a time published a local newspaper named *Atish*. In one edition, writing about Urdu poetry with foreign connections, he mentioned Balthazar Bourbon's love for Urdu poetry.

Dr Ram Babu Saksena saved some of Balthazar's poetry from oblivion. Dr Ram Babu was a member of the Uttar Pradesh Civil Service. He was the appointed administrator of the then Tonk State. Known as a father of Urdu language, he was very well respected in Bhopal, too. Ajaz Masih Bourbon, son of Bonaventura Bourbon, gave a collection of Balthazar's poetry to Raja Avad Narayan Bisaria, Prime Minister of Bhopal.

The two volumes of Balthazar Bourbon's poetry, one in Farsi and the other in Urdu, were then passed on to Dr Ram Babu Saksena. The Urdu *dewan* (collection of poetry) consists of 66 pages and is not complete. The paper is thick yellow, aged, and frayed at the edges owing to decay. There are also *ghazal*s written on the margin but many are not completely decipherable because of the torn edges. The *takhullous* (pen name) Fitrat appears on the pages every now and then in this manuscript. Many pages are missing from the book in the beginning. There are eight *muqadmas* (introduction and translation with explanation) at the end of the *ghazals*. The first is of Hafiz's *ghazals*, but the verses of Fitrat are in Urdu. Dr Ram Babu Saksena writes, 'there is no doubt that Fitrat is a poet of high order. He has thorough command over the language and is well versed in the technique of poetry. He employs various artifices and figures of speech to show his mastery over the language and verse forms. His verses have a compactness, neatness and flow and are marked by a felicity of diction and harmony of numbers. The influence of the Lucknow school of Nasikh's poetry is occasionally reflected in some of the verses (Saksena 1941, 211).

Dr Saksena writes that Fitrat has also written in difficult meters with stiff rhymes and double rhymes, which were in vogue during those times. Undoubtedly, his position as an Urdu and Persian poet and his *dewan* is high amongst Anglo Indian poets. Saksena writes, 'He can also be considered along good second class Urdu Poets.' The Farsi *dewan* by Fitrat is also incomplete. Dr Saksena had also seen some 354 scattered pages entitled *Taimur Nama* (Biography of Taimur), at the end of which is a stamped seal. These *dewans* of Fitrat have been untraced and no book has quoted even one line. Even his poetic pen-name was not correctly known.

I was able to retrieve and translate a few verses:

Paaya na ho Buland kyon uske Kalaam ka,
Wasif Jo ho Massey Alay Hus Salam ka.

Why shouldn't the status of his poetry be high,
Of the person who is a follower of Jesus (the Prophet)
peace be upon him.

Shaikh ji Toor pe chamki thi Bijli jiski,
Apne butkhane me hum wahi sanam rakhte Hain.

The lightning that was there at the time of Moses at the mountain, I keep the idol of that God in my heart.

Jeene de mujhe Jaan ka aahang na kar tu,
Ae hasrate dil itna bhi ab tung na kar tu.

Let me live, don't you care for life,
O my heart don't trouble me so much now.

Hota hai paragand dimage gule rana,
Bas zamzamaye marge band aahna na kar tu.

My lovely flower (She) will be disturbed (distressed),
While dying, just don't quiver or cry.

Is arz-e-purnoor ko har baar dikhakar,
Aaina hairat ko bohat tang na kar tu.

After showing such a beautiful face time and again,
Don't trouble the mirror or surprise (me) so much.

Fitrat wo mujhse jaan ka khwahan hai in dinon,
Adna si shai ke waste inkar kya karun?

Fitrat (pen-name) now-a-days she is willing for my life,
For such a small thing, how can I refuse?

Dikha jhazbe mohabbat ka es qadar taseer,
Uodu ki bazm say uthke voh mare ghar aya.

I saw the extent of my love,
She left the side of my rival and came to my house.

Jo chahra daikh lay us mahajabinka,
Tha sthuk chand hoya chodavain ka.

If you have seen the face of that lady,
You have seen the full moon on the sky.

Khafa us bath par hua mujhsay woh,
Jho liya tha bhosa zulfha ambre ka.

She is annoyed now with me,
Because I kissed her beautiful scented hair.

Lipta hue khak who ke main damansa yar kha,
Yae sach hai marthba hai bara khaksar ka.

I have on my lap the dust on which my love walked,
This makes my stature high.

Ejazat mangthi hai sozishe dil,
Lagha dho agh aahe pur shareer sah.

The itch in my heart (of love) wants the permission,
To burn my whole body.

Garmi se is nigah ki dil kis tarah na pighle,
Aaina aab hokar hairat se bah gaya tha.

Why should not the heart melt with the warmth
of her gaze,
The surprised mirror had turned into water
and flown away.

Hargiz na koi aise zulmon sitam sahega,
Yah mai hi tha ki kya kya kuchh zor sah gaya tha.

No one would suffer such unkindness in love,
It was me alone who stood such cruelty.

Bahana is qadar aansu ke bah jaave sabhi aalam,
Na karna mujhko hamchashmon me tu e chashmtar jhoota.

Oh, my eyes weep such tears that may drown
the world,
Don't put me to shame my moist eyes in
her company.

Dile sangi me iske kuchh na kuchh taseer kar baithe,
Ilahi nalaye dil ka na ho jaye asar jhoota.

Let her heart be moved by the flint of my sighs,
Oh God; See not my sighs go in vain.

Balthazar's death and the mystery of his grave

Balthazar died on 1 January 1829. It is believed that he was poisoned. Madam Dulhan Sahib, his wife, used to say that he vomited before dying and the spittoon, which has the name Sarkar Bibi Sahiba or Dulhan Sahib inscribed on it, turned green due to poison.

Ugaldan (spittoon) of Sardar Bibi, alias Dulhan Sahib, used by Shahzad Masih before his death Source: Author's private collection

Many books say that Balthzar was buried in civil lines, Agra, and 'a handsome red tomb is built there'.[8] This untrue statement resulted in many people searching in vain for his grave in all the Christian graveyards of Agra. Magdaline Bourbon's family picture of Balthazar had a note written behind it stating that Balthazar was buried in Bhopal in front of Bhopal Talkies (an old cinema theatre). There was a graveyard there called Isai Ganj, or Christian place. To give the 500 Christians who came to Bhopal with Salvador Bourbon their burial rights, the Begums had given land for a Christian cemetery. There were around 300 graves on the land, as well as a small church. The Bourbons looked after the cemetery. When Balthazar died, this charge was given to his wife, Madam Dulhan Sahib.

The Begums thought that because all the Bourbons are buried in the Christian cemetery, Balthazar would find a place there as well. However, this was not true. Looking for more evidence linked to the back of the family picture of Balthazar on which is written a statement citing Balthazar's grave in the Muslim graveyard near a famous film theatre in Bhopal,

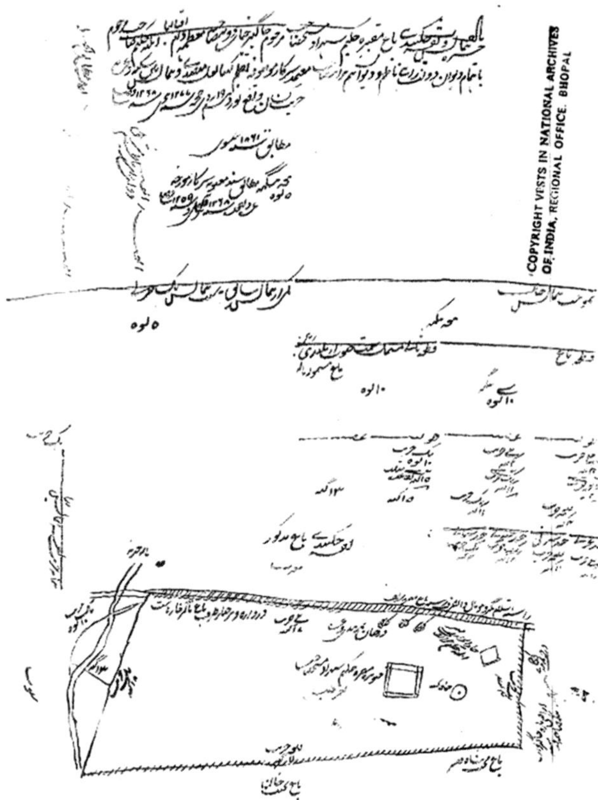

Map of the graveyard showing the grave of Balthazar Bourbon, alias Shehzad Masih, and his father, Salvador, marked with a square. The circle is a baoli (step well) that is still there. The smaller square is the grave of the wife of John Sahab. Below (i.e. on the east side) is the garden of Muhubbat Shah Faqir and Najib Khan. This map is from 1861 Source: National Archives of Bhopal

I came across a map of the graveyard where the grave of Shahzad Masih is located. In the meantime, I met a local historian, Rizwan Uddin Ansari, who is a descendent of Mianji Muhammed Riaz Uddin Ansari, a trustee of Nawab Qudisa Begum, friend of Hakim Shahzad Masih, and teacher of Nawab Sikandar Jahan Begum. By studying maps from the National Archive, Rizwan Uddin Ansari was able to locate the exact place of the grave. Mianji Riaz Uddin Ansari, confidant and *Kamdar* (Prime Minister) of Qudsia Begum, sketched one of the maps in 1861 and other in 1862 to solve a despute related to land owned by members of the Bourbon family. Hakim Shahzad Masih owned a piece of land called Bara

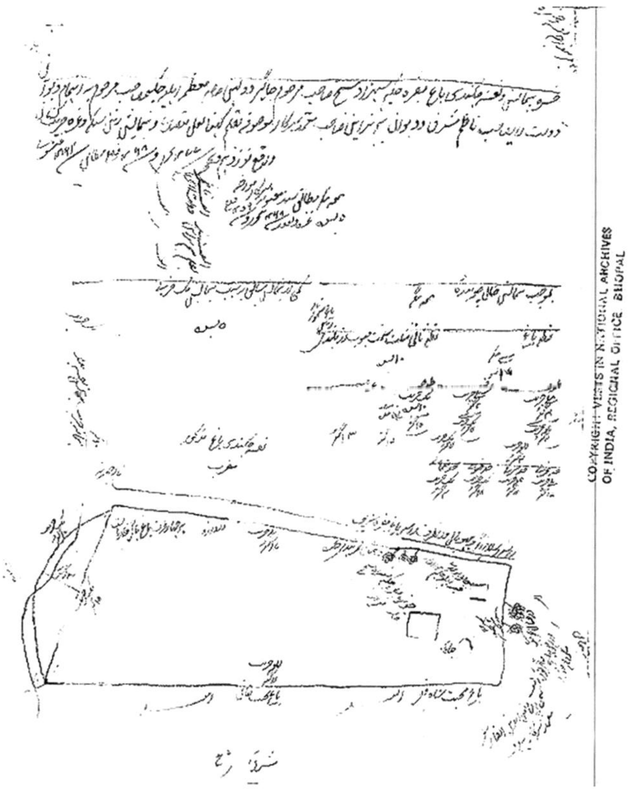

Map of the graves in the garden of Shahzad Masih (now a Muslim graveyard), prepared in 1862 by Mianji Muhammad Riaz Uddin Ansari, confidant and *Kamdar* (Prime Minister) of Nawab Qudsia Begum and colleague of Shahzad Masih Source: National Archives of Bhopal

Bagh, or The Big Garden. The land was given to him by Nawab Qudsia Begum. The dispute was around a wall built for partition that was disrupting the main road. Bhopal residents complained to Nawab Qudsia Begum. She appointed Riaz Uddin Ansari to investigate into this property matter, which was soon settled because of the good relations between Begum Qudsia and Madam Dulhan. This is according to documents about Dulhan Sahib from the Sanad and Jagir Section in the National Archives.

In the garden of Hakim Shahzad Masih now stands a Muslim graveyard behind Pagoda Hotel, Hamidia Road, Bhopal. Mr Ansari knew from his family about the grave of Shahzad Masih, as described by his grandfather. Mr Ansari mentioned that with the grave of Hakim Shahzad Masih were three more graves. One is the grave of his father, Inayat Masih, and the other two are the graves of Shahzad Masih's sisters. After many decades, it is hard to locate the graves of the sisters, which suggests that they were less grand. The graves of Hakim Shahzad Masih and Inayat Masih are still there. These two graves are on an erected platform; the graves of the sisters were flat, but on the same platform. As told by Mr Ansari, there was a stone railing encircling each of the two graves. The platform and the design engraved on it are the same as those on the graves of rulers of that time such as Nawab Siddiq Hasan Khan and Nawab Shahjahan Begum, though the railing is higher for the graves of the Nawabs. It was also mentioned in the map that a tomb was to be erected on these graves, but this idea was later dropped. The deep well mentioned in one of the maps is now

Graves of the Bourbons

Bottom: Grave of Bathazar Bourbon (Shahzad Masih), and his father, Salvador Bourbon (Inayat Masih), on the raised platform Source: Author's private collection

covered with mud but has some water. The grave of the wife of John Sahab mentioned on the same map can still be found, but is difficult to reach due to shrubs and mud.

Endnotes

1. Sanad and Jagir file no 514/1 Inayat Masih, National Archives of India, Bhopal.

2. There is more definitive information regarding Philip Bourbon, alias Imdad Masih, marrying Mary Smith, with whom he had five daughters. Four died young. The fifth, Isabelle, married a Mr Johannes.

3. Sanad and Jagir file no 514/1 Inayat Masih, National Archives of India, Bhopal.

4. Tazia are miniature mausoleums of Karbala, generally made of coloured paper, bamboo, tin foil, mica, and glass. Thousands of tazia in various shapes and sizes are fashioned every year for the Muharram month of mourning.

5. Sanad and Jagir files, National Archives of India, Bhopal.

6. The Pereiras were a French family who settled in Pondicherry, a French Colony. Colonel Joseph Pereira came to India in 1801. His son, Manuel Pereira, later became a Captain in the Bhopal State army and married Matthew De Silva's daughter, Joana, who was Portuguese.

7. Written by Sayyid Abdu'-Latif, published by London: Forster Groom Co. Limited 15, Charing Cross, S.W.1.

8. *Taj ul Iqbal Tarikh Bhopal* by Shah Jahan Begum, translated by H. C. Barstow, Calcutta: 1876, p. 39.

THE HEROIC ACTS OF MADAM DULHAN AND HER ADOPTED SON, SEBASTIAN BOURBON

Dulhan Sahib, wife of Balthazar Bourbon
Source: Author's private collection

Amongst the Bourbons, one of the most fascinating characters was Dulhan Sahib, wife of Balthazar Bourbon (Shahzad Masih). One of the earliest accounts of Madame de Bourbon was narrated by Louis Rousselet whose travelogue, *India and its Native Princes*, describes his meeting with the Bourbons in Bhopal. During his visit to Bhopal, he met with a Catholic priest who, surprisingly, addressed him in French. The priest mentioned that he served as a chaplain to Madame Elizabeth de Bourbon, whom he invited Rousselet to meet. Rousselet listened to the priest 'without being able to believe [his] ears' (Rousselet [1875] 1975, 453). He decided to accept the opportunity to meet Madame de Bourbon, who had been given a stature like that of a princess in Muslim Bhopal. Rousselet was sent an elephant to meet the Bourbon Sirdar (Princess Bourbon) who, as described by Rousselet, 'was very rich, possessed important fiefs and held high rank among the great vassals of the crown' (Ibid.). Rousselet 'was struck by her type, which is eminently European, and by the clear yellow tint of her skin' (Ibid., 454).

Madam Dulhan

In 1821, Balthazar Bourbon married the daughter of a Captain Johnstone from the Bengal army, whose own wife was of Pathan origin.[1] Kincaid (1887, 173) narrates the following story of this couple: Captain Johnstone and his wife had a son and a daughter. The son was sent to England for further education. Johnstone's wife did not want to send her daughter, Elizabeth, to England, so she fled to Hyderabad for protection and stayed with relatives. When Qudsia Begum sent a mission to find Balthazar Bourbon a wife, Elizabeth was only 11 years old, but she and her mother were asked to go to Bhopal. Elizabeth, having been identified as a suitable English lady, married Balthazar Bourbon in 1821 and changed her name to Isabella Bourbon. The royal family of Bhopal gave her the title of Dulhan Sahib. When foreigners used to visit Bhopal they used to refer to her as Madam Dulhan.

A few sources from the National Archives[2] reflect a different story about Madam Dulhan's lineage. These documents suggest that Isabella was the daughter of a Muslim woman entertainer from Kanpur. It is further written that Hakim Shahzad Masih brought her to Bhopal to serve his mother when she was 12 (15), and later married her, probably in the year 1825

(1821). She was only 18 (21) when Shahzad Masih died in 1829. There were no proper records during those days and thus the ambiguity with the dates and her age.

The family photos of Dulhan Sahib depict her Pathan origin and her style of dress shows that she is of royal lineage. This evidence suggests that Kincaid's (1887) narrative is more accurate and, indeed, the more popular story is that Balthazar's wife was a daughter of Captain Johnstone, that she was later given the title Dulhan Sahib, and that after marriage her name was changed to Isabella de Bourbon.

Balthazar died in 1829. It is said that the Pathans poisoned him because of the Bourbons' proximity to the royal family. Dulhan Sahib was with Balthazar during his last days. After his death, Dulhan Sahib was made responsible for about 500 Christians residing in Bhopal State. With this new responsibility her titled was changed to Sarkar Dulhan. She was given a *jagir* of Rs. 86,000 by Sikandar Begum. She also served as Lady in Waiting, to the Begum. Dulhan Sahib had a special charge—to look after young Shahjahan, who would be the next ruler of Bhopal. In one of Shahjahan's letters, she addressed Dulhan Sahib as '*Meri pyari Chachi*' (my beloved Aunt). After her husband Balthazar's death, Dulhan Sahib played the important role of matriarch of the Bourbon clan and leader of the Christian community in Bhopal. Dulhan Sahib was among the few trusted confidants of Qudsia Begum and her lifestyle was also very much like the Begums.

Dulhan Sahib sitting and smoking a hookah, attended by her servants
Source: Author's private collection

Isabella Bourbon was known for loyal service, courage, fidelity, and steadfastness.[3] Isabella had one daughter, Joanna Budhan, alias Bibi Huria. She also adopted as her own Sebastian, the son of a Brahmin lady from Ichhawar. This Brahmin lady claimed that Sebastian's father was Balthazar Bourbon, though he was born posthumously and there are no records about the background of this lady or how she came into contact with Shahzad Masih. There is a rumour that some people were taking a lady for *sati* (a now obsolete Hindu funeral custom where a widow burns to death on the pyre of her husband), and Shahzad Masih intervened to stop this from happening. He then brought her back with him and asked her to stay in his outhouse. Later, a relationship developed between them but he never married her. After Balthazar's death, it is said that Balthazar's cousin Dominick Bourbon[4] and Balthazar's servant, Fazil Khan, brought this boy from Ichhawar to Dulhan

Sahib and claimed he was Balthazar's son. Dulhan Sahib considered their claim and adopted him.

Dulhan Sahib lived in a special palace named after her, Dulhan Sahib Mahal. She had many servants, including Abyssinian slaves, who were maintained by the *mansab* (financial help) she received from the royal family. Dulhan Sahib Mahal was situated in Lakherapura, right behind Yasin Mahal (i.e. on its eastern side), adjacent to the Masjid of Muhi Uddin Ansari and Imam Bara. The main gate was said to have been quite high, about 16 feet or so, so an elephant with a rider could easily pass below it. The height of one's gate was a symbol of affluence in those days. The palace was a two-storey building in an area of about one acre, with a huge courtyard at the centre.

Top: Ivory *Itr daan* (dainty small box to keep Indian perfume) of Dulhan Sahib

Bottom: Decorated legs of the bed of Dulhan Sahib
Source: Author's private collection

Construction of Jehangirabad Church

After Balthazar's demise, Dulhan Sahib was made responsible for the Christian community in Bhopal. Dulhan Sahib met her responsibilities with full devotion. During the time of Salvador and Balthazar Bourbon, priests had been sent from Agra and Nagpur to conduct Catholic services for the Bourbons in Bhopal. Balthazar, later in his life, had a resident chaplain in his palace (Saksena 1941, 203). Upon Balthazar's death, Father Constance Fernandez, the resident chaplain, went to Gwalior and became chaplain of the Filose family. From 1840 to 1860 Vicars Apostolic kept sending a priest to visit Bhopal.

In 1851, Father Bernard visited Bhopal and Madam Dulhan promised him part of her garden to construct a church. The garden was situated one mile from the palace, where her husband Balthazar and other Bourbons are buried (Ibid.). However, there was no follow-up regarding the construction of the church after Father Bernard's visit.

Front and inner views of St. Francis Church, constructed by Sebastian Bourbon in 1873 on land given by Dulhan Sahib
Source: Author's private collection

In 1861, Sikandar Begum started a tour of India. With her travelled the ladies of the Bourbon family, including Madam Dulhan. In Agra, Madam Dulhan met with the Bishop of Agra. She requested that he send a chaplain to reside in Bhopal and look after the Christians there. She also promised to build a church, and to give suitable land for the priest to stay, along with a salary of Rs. 100 per month. It took 10 years, however, for a suitable residence to be built for the Christian priests. Upon requests from Madam Dulhan, Father Raphael and Father Norbat were sent to Bhopal by the Agra Bishop. Shahjahan Begum formally donated the land for Bhopal Catholic Church to Isabella Bourbon (Madame Dulhan) in 1873. The Sultan Jahan Begum granted permission to build the church on the condition that it should be outside city limits. At that time, Pulpukta Bridge was the municipal boundary and Jehangirabad was outside the city limits.

Sebastian Bourbon built the church in Jehangirabad. A monthly grant of Rs. 70 was given by the State towards its maintenance. The site consisted of a small church and a house for the priest, and the church opened for services in 1875. The construction of this church marked the beginning of formally recognized Christianity in Bhopal. Rt. Dr Paul Tosi blessed the Church and it was open for prayers to the Christian population. The church was like the old churches, with thick walls. It was different, though, because it had a curtain in the middle of the prayer room to divide the room so the women could be in *purdah* like their Muslim peers. Strict *purdah* was observed in the church; women sat on one side of the curtain, men on the other. My mother Magdeline de Bourbon, a very shy person, came out of *purdah* for the first time during her wedding.

The Bourbons were supposed to pay for the upkeep of the priest, but when the *jagir*s of the Bourbons were interrupted (there were occasional lapses between these gifts) the Begums covered these gaps by paying the priests from State revenue. Up to now, the government pays Rs. 70 per month to the priest of the Catholic Cathedral in Bhopal. The Archaeology Department has declared the Bhopal Cathedral a heritage building.

Bottom: The altar inside St. Francis Church, Bhopal

Bottom Right: Bourbon graves inside St. Francis Church, Bhopal, including that of Isabella Bourbon (Dulhan Sahib) Source: Author's private collection

Like the Begums, the Bourbons spoke Urdu, and their food habits and customs were just like those of Bhopali Muslims. Sardar Bahu, alias Miss Bernard, wife of Sebastian Bourbon, wore traditional attire such as *kurta*s (long shirts) that were fitted on the sides, folded at the waist, and draped down like a frock with *churidar pyjama*s (tights) They wore these with neatly pleated contrasting colour *dupatta*s (scarves) about four yards long. This style of dress was very peculiar to Bhopal.

Sebastian Bourbon's wife, Miss Bernard, wearing traditional Bhopali attire Source: Author's private collection Note: Also see picture of a Bhopali lady on p.19.

Behind the church, the Begums had given orders to construct a palace. The land up to the foot of the mountain was the *jagir* of the Bourbons. Behind the Jehangirabad Haveli (palace) was Motia Talao (a pond). On Saturdays, the fisherman there used to cook fish by covering it with wet mud, and later baking it over a fire of dry twigs. The cooked fish was served as dinner for the Bourbons. During the summer season, mango trees were the main attraction. Rope swings hung from the trees for the ladies to enjoy this leisure activity. The Bourbon family used to travel from Lakherapura in bullock carts on Saturdays, stay the night, and leave on Sunday evenings. The bullock carts were covered from all sides to maintain privacy for the Bourbon women.

Beyond practising *purdah*, the Bourbons adopted other customs that were not common among other Christians. For instance, on Maundy Thursday during the holy week of Lent (the month for fasting), a ritual was performed in which the oldest male member of the family used to wash the feet of 12 men. After this, each of the 12 men were presented with a clean new towel with a wrapped piece of unleavened bread. This was done in commemoration of Jesus Christ. The priest also performed this ritual in the church. After the prayers were completed, the whole family sat around and ate *roti* (Indian bread) made of gram flour (*besan*) and a special dish made from eggplant, known as *'baingan ka bhurtha'*. The peculiar thing about this dish was that it contained no *ghee* (clarified butter) or oil, though other Christians, then and now, do not stipulate avoidance of these ingredients for such a meal.

A cemetery, known as Isai Ganj (the Christian place) and a school were also built near the church. The patron of the church is St. Francis. The feast of St. Francis falls on 3 December every year. The Bourbons started commemorating it by holding a ceremony my mother called the Malidha Festival. On 3 December, she would call all of us and make us sit on a carpet, upon which a clean white sheet was placed. The ritual of making *'malidha'* would begin by first making sure that our hands and nails were clean. The elders would make thick *puri*s like small round thin pancakes, made from *atta* (wheat flour). The flour was well kneaded with pure *ghee* specially brought for the occasion. Once this was done, our task was to crush the puris into powder (the literal meaning of *malidha* is crushing to make powder). One portion of this powder would go the priest of the church and another would be blessed and brought to the house as *prasad* (blessed offering).

Although Jehangirabad church was used as the burial ground for a few members of the Bourbon family, including Isabella, Sebastian, and his wife, Veronica Bourbon (known as Miss Joanna Bernard before marriage), the rest of the Christians of that era are buried in the Catholic Cemetery on Berasia Road, the oldest Catholic cemetery in Bhopal. Catholic Church records show that there were about 300 hundred graves there, including those of the Bourbons.

After Balthazar's death in 1829, Sikandar Begum's husband, Nawab Jahangir Muhammad Khan, tried to kill her to gain possession of Bhopal State. She somehow managed to escape, and Madam Dulhan and Sebastian Bourbon accompanied Sikandar Begum and her mother, Qudsia Begum, to take refuge in the fort of Islam Nagar. During this time, Nawab Jahangir Muhammad Khan and Asad Ali Khan (the then Prime Minister) were slowly removing officers and other people loyal to Qudsia Begum and Sikandar Begum. Many continued to serve Qudsia Begum, though, despite her inability at that time to pay them much. She did manage to compensate those loyal to her with a portion of the *jagir* she still owned. Dulhan Sahib and the Bourbons also suffered financial losses when Asad Ali Khan started to take possession of her properties, which were valued at around Rs. 86,000 at that time. Asad Ali ultimately did manage to gain control of all properties, including Ichhawar. Sikandar Begum tried her best to get the property back to Dulhan Sahib, who remained with her all that time, but her plea fell on deaf ears.

Madam Dulhan remained with the Begums during all the trying years that followed, until the death of Jahangir Muhammad Khan in 1844. At that point, the Begums were safe and returned to Bhopal from the Islam Nagar fort. Sikandar Begum's first act on being appointed Regent was to restore to the Bourbon family the lands confiscated by the Nawab Jahangir. She retained Madam Dulhan and her adopted son at her court. Shahjahan Begum, who became ruler of Bhopal after Sikandar Begum, was born in Islam Nagar, shortly after the ladies fled from there. Since Madam Dulhan was the most trusted, she was given charge of the young princess. Sarkar Dulhan herself died at the age of 80, on 29 Ramdan 1299 A.H. (03 June 1882 AD), one year after the passing away of Qudsia Begum.

The reign of the Begums was the most fruitful period for Bhopal. In these two centuries, Bhopal State prospered and the Begums worked on the provision of basic amenities including clean drinking water, railways, post offices, and the construction of structures such as the beautiful palace of Shaukat Mahal and other landmark buildings. The Indo-French architecture of Bhopal had become world famous. Bhopal also pioneered women's education with its beautiful libraries. The peaceful rule of the Begums was characterized by a beautiful blend of Hindu and Muslim cultures, which made Bhopal unique in many ways. To this day, Bhopal is known for its *Ganga–Jamuni tehzeeb*, which signifies the marriage between India's dominant cultures.

Sebastian Bourbon

Balthazar Bourbon's son, Sebastian Bourbon, alias Meherban Masih (1830–1878), was appointed Prime

Minister to Sikandar Begum in 1857. During this time, Sebastian became chief architect of one of the most beautiful palaces in Bhopal, Shaukat Mahal. Sebastian also built Lakerapura Palace for his mother, Madam Dulhan, and championed the construction of Bhopal Catholic Church.

Like his predecessors, Sebastian continued to protect the Begums from internal assassination plots and treason, and he continued the family legacy of communicating effectively with the British on behalf of the Begums. He was 17 years of age when he married Miss Bernard, daughter of Captain Bernard of Sardhana, in 1847. She was a cousin on the mother's side of the Filose family.

Sebastian Bourbon's greatest service was in 1857, when he was indispensable as an adviser, commander of the Bhopal army and Captain of the city. Sebastian and his mother rendered Nawab Sikandar Begum such invaluable service that this lion-hearted woman was able to suppress all attempts at rebellion within Bhopal State during a time of tremendous risk and uncertainty in and around Bhopal.

Top: Dulhan Sahib with her son, Sebastian Bourbon

Bottom: Miss Bernard, wife of Sebastian Bourbon
Source: Author's private collection

The role of Dulhan Sahib, Sebastian Bourbon, and Bhopal Christians in the 1857 Uprising

'In India one is always sitting on a volcano.'
—Lord Dalhousie, Governor-General of India, 1848 (Peers 2013, 66)

The Indian Rebellion of 1857 is called by many names, including The Revolt of 1857, The First War of Indian Independence, The Indian Uprising, The Great Rebellion, The Sepoy Rebellion and The Sepoy Mutiny. Historians do agree, however, that the situation came extremely close to suddenly and permanently ending British imperialism in India. It started when sepoys refused to touch the gunpowder cartridges sent to India for the new Enfield rifles with which the East India Company troops were being equipped. The cartridges were greased with beef and pig fat, and loading the rifles required tearing open those greased cartridges with one's teeth—which insulted both Hindu and Muslim religious practices. In India, cows are sacred, and for Muslims, using any part of a pig is against Islam. A small group of sepoys refused their orders, calling it a rebellion against the East India Company.

On 29 March 1857, Mangal Pandey, a Hindu sepoy of the 34th Bengal Native Infantry, attacked some British officers at the Barrackpore parade ground. The regiment was later disbanded and the rebellious soldiers sentenced to death by hanging. The next major incident was in the cantonment of the town of Meerut. This escalated into other civilian rebellions when Hindu and Muslim peasants and landlords also joined the uprising, which ultimately spread to the Upper Gangetic Plain and to Central India, with the major conflicts in Uttar Pradesh, western Bihar, northern Madhya Pradesh, and Delhi. The majority of the Indian population did not join the uprising, but historians agree that the fighting was brutal. Of the 40,000 Europeans living in India that year, approximately one in seven perished. On the Indian side, at least 800,000 died in the uprising (Peers 2013, 64).

The Bhopal rebels were initially encouraged by Qudsia Begum and Dulhan Sahib, who provided the rebels of Indore with financial and moral support to continue their fight against the British. This continued until Sikandar Begum, wrote a stiff admonitory letter to her mother, explaining the dire consequences. After reading the letter, Qudsia Begum stopped financing the rebels. Surrounded on every side by hostile neighbours such as the Marathas at Indore and Gwalior, Rajputs in Rajasthan, and even the Nizam in the Deccan, Sikandar Begum had vowed loyalty to the emerging forces of the East India Company.

The code sign of the Uprising, '*roti*' (Indian flat bread), became a symbol of the first freedom movement and started uniting the people to fight against the British. In August 1856, greased cartridge production was initiated by the British at Fort William, Calcutta. The Indian firm of Gangadarh Banerji & Co supplied the grease that was used. The ruling Begum, Sikandar Jahan, heard news about the distribution of rotis among the army of Meerut. Munshi Bhawani Prasad, State lawyer to Sikandar Jahan Begum, reported the news to her, describing unrest that had started at Neemach in June 1857, and how things were getting worse in the Holkar State (now Indore).

Sikandar Jahan Begum started to prepare for the events to come. She sent a letter to the British political agents in Indore regarding the safety of the English army. Colonel Durand was sure she could be trusted, but she also assured the political agent Major W. H. Richards of her loyalty. The Nawab sent a convoy that comprised of 270 men as well as two *risala*s of 600 cavalry and 400 infantry to help the British at Indore. The Indore cantonment was the first to revolt in Central India and they murdered several Europeans. Colonel Durand, after handing over the keys of the treasury[5] and the magazine (guns and cartridges) to the Begum's trusted military leader Murawwat Mohd Khan, retreated safely with a British group of 17 men and 11 ladies to Hoshangabad Fort[6] with 30 mounted soldiers and 50 on foot under the command of a *risaldar* (commander of a mounted troop). The fort was protected by a loyal Pathan contingent. This group included Mr William Ray and Major Richards.

Now Sikandar Jahan Begum was the sole in charge of all the forces. She ordered the safety of all the bungalows and the treasury. This was the time when the Indian rulers of Bhopal State could have asked for independence—but they were deeply under the influence of the foreigners. Sikandar Jahan Begum issued letters to Nawab Qudsia Begum, Molvi Mohammad Saaduddin, and collectors of eastern, western, and southern districts to dispatch army troops for protection of Sehore. She requested guards and local merchants, as well. She also wrote to Dulhan Sahib Bourbon to be cautious about her ornaments and jewellery, and be ready to reach Bhopal when summoned. She wrote to Mohammad Raza Husain, acting Prime Minister of Bhopal State, inquiring whether Abdul Qayyum, *Daroga* (Guardian) of Fatehgarh Fort, had received a notice from Cawnpore (now called Kanpur) regarding interference of the British Government in the religious affairs of the Indians. Abdul Qayyum, in his response, denied receiving any such notice. Colonel James Travers prepared to leave Bhopal for Indore, but expressed the necessity of strict vigilance over the movements of the army contingent of Bhopal.

Sikandar Jahan Begum tried her best to safeguard the Europeans, against the wishes of her agitated subjects; the Muslim landowners and rest of the public were not in favour of the British. She remained calm and foresighted, and kept an eye on all the events in Bhopal and supported the British in all possible ways. She dispatched two persons to Bhilsa and Shahjahanpur for collecting news. Dulhan Sahib was responsible for the safety of Ichhawar. Dulhan Sahib reported panic in the business community of Ichhawar due to activities of Indian insurgents there. She was in constant touch with the Begum, reporting the conditions of Ichhawar daily. Nawab Sikandar Jahan Begum gave orders to Sabit Mohammad Khan Jagirdar to proceed to Raisen, and he kept sending reports about the situation there. It was expected that rebels from Indore might come to Sehore; Bakshi Bahadur Mohammad Khan was given the charge to intercept any mutineers. Murawwat Mohd was sent with two companies to ensure the security of Sehore, and Munshi Bhawani Prasad was asked to stay there to help.

Sikandar Jahan Begum banned the sale of lead and explosives across Bhopal State. She also ordered the submission of arms from certain people. She arranged enough firepower for the forces and ensured a strict vigil on its distribution and usage. She was insistent that mutineers of Bhopal State or other regions must not be helped if they arrived in Bhopal. Some merchants started to move from Sehore to Bhopal for fear of being looted by the insurgents. Seeing this, the Begum increased security for the local businessman. *Moulvi*s (Muslim religious leaders) in the city were preaching for *jihad*, and used to gather at Masjid Manka Shah and Masjid Madar ul Muham. Hatred against the English was so much that laymen were reluctant to serve them and even the Nawab's own forces were threatening her. Most of the disturbances were in the southern districts, near Hoshangabad, about 200 kilometers from Bhopal, and the Nawab was expecting trouble from that side. She appointed someone for getting information from Hoshangabad. Nawab Baqi Mohammad Khan was her adviser and kept an eye on all state affairs. Nawab Sikandar Jahan came to know from her sources that Fazil Mohammad Khan, great-grandson of Dost Mohammad Khan, and Adil Mohammad Khan, the *jagirdar*s of Amba Pani, were supporting the rebels.

On 1 July 1857, Nawab Sikandar Jahan Begum wrote to all the Hindu and Muslim residents of Bhopal State and advised them not to pay attention to the rumours of interference by the British government in religious affairs, asking them to cooperate with her and obey her orders. She urged the residents not to join hands with Muslim rebels. There were reports about the designs of Fazil Mohammad Khan and Wazir Ullah Khan to destroy Sehore after capturing the guns of the Bhopal army contingent. There was also news about the advent of 25 armed persons from Bundelkhand to Sheikhpura, and the determination of Fazil Mohammad Khan to kill the commander and deputy of the Bhopal army. By this time, Nawab Sikandar Jahan Begum's treasury was nearly empty and she could not afford any extra expenses, so she asked Nawab Baqi Mohammad Khan, Nawab Qudsia Begum, Nawab Muiz Mohammad Khan, Dulhan Sahib, and Foujdar Mohammad Khan to arrange for a loan from the local merchants at a 1 per cent interest rate. Nawab Qudsia Begum assured her of assistance but advised her to be careful in spending the money. Jean de Silva informed Dulhan Sahib that he had arranged a loan from the local merchants which would be given to her for the Begum.[7]

On 3 July 1857, a group of British officers coming from Sehore reached Ichhawar, where Dulhan Sahib was ready to welcome them and provided much needed rest and protection. They were then escorted to Hoshangabad for safety, along with Qazi Syed Gouhar Ali and 30 mounted soldiers led by Sebastian Bourbon, who had helped foil a dangerous massacre plot against these British troops. If the massacre had taken place, it would have antagonized the British against the Begums. Sikandar Begum rode with Sebastian to the military parade ground near Jehangirabad. There the Begum distributed gold coins to each of her soldiers in an appeal for their loyalty; she announced that she would never survive her own soldiers' disloyalty.

Another group of British men, women and children arrived from Indore, seeking refuge at Aunchor,

Jaora; this group included Captain Carter from Agra, Captain McDougal, McPherson, Dr Selphint, Captain Lamar Shunt, Ekfield, Madame Barton, Madame Harrison, Mr White, Madame Holmen, and their children. Jean de Silva and several of the Bourbon family who were then residing in Jehangirabad, Bhopal, provided hospitality and shelter to Christian fugitives of the 1857 Uprising.[8] After reaching Hoshangabad, Mr William Ray wrote a document stating: 'We reached here safely in which Qazi Syed Gouhar Ali and Sebastian Bourbon had done excellent arrangement during the way and we are happy with them.' Qazi Hanif Mohammad of Doraha also gave assurance of his loyalty to the Begum.

The unrest continued. There were reports of local soldiers, who were against the Begums, creating disturbances in the market by assaulting a Bohra Muslim shopkeeper and other merchants, mixing bone-dust in the sugar and ghee, making it impure for vegetarians. Sikandar Jahan Begum ordered the examination of the sugar and found the allegation was true in some cases. In July, Murawwat Mohammad Khan sent a report to Nawab Sikandar Jahan Begum stating, 'Yesterday in Ram Lila ground in the presence of all the officers of the contingent, Ganesh Ram, Mohtamim of the Judicial and criminal department, and Madan Mohan, Naib Vakil, the suspected sugar was examined and found to contain bone-dust.' On the same day, Nawab Qudsia Begum requested that Nawab Sikandar Jahan Begum post her troops at Islam Nagar because there was danger of an attack on Bhopal by the rebel forces of Mhow.

Many rumours were spreading in those days: Raja Shah Garh willing to pay higher rates, Maharaj Holkar of Indore State killing many white men, shopkeepers selling sugar with bone residue, use of fat in the bullets, etc. The officials of the Bhopal contingent sent a request to the Begum that the stock of sugar sent by the merchants should be destroyed, as it was likely to create trouble. However, Raza Husain inspected the entire stock and found the allegations by the acting Prime Minister to be false. Raza Husain recommended that entire stock be purchased by the State so there was no loss of the merchants. Non-commissioned officers such as Mahavir, Majju Lal, Wali Shah, and his brother, Arif Shah, continued to instigate the people by distributing derogatory pamphlets. They even collected a few Pindaris and formed their own court and government by the name of 'Sipahi Bahadur'.

On 14 July 1857, Kamdar Khan Pindari joined his brother Shuja'at Khan with 70 followers and attacked the British garrison in Berasia with a force of 400 men. They managed to kill Subha Rao, the assistant political agent; Makhdum Baksh, a merchant; a peon, and a sepoy. They also burnt the bungalow and took control of the treasury. John Jacob Francis, Jamadar of Police at Berasia, was later charged and orders were issued for his arrest for the plunder and killing. Jacob was arrested on 14 March 1858, and General Rose issued orders to hang him. He was hanged in public. His wife was given Rs. 100 and his father's existing grant was renewed. Dulhan Sahib supported him to get this grant.

Nawab Sikandar Jahan Begum issued orders to ban the sale and purchase of lead and gunpowder across the city. The Begum wrote to the political agent in Bhopal that the Hindus and Muslims of the State prefer that the English do not meddle with their State's affairs. The number of the rebels was rising and the Bhopal treasury did not have enough finances to curb the many revolts. The British refused to pay for the Bhopal army's expenses. However, there was continued support from Qudsia Begum for Nawab Sikandar Jahan Begum's efforts to stop unrest in the state. Qudsia Begum even paid the army from her personal treasury, as she strongly believed that the army must be paid to acknowledge their sacrifices. The Begums believed that everybody must work in the army willingly and anyone who wanted to go must be allowed to go. Qudsia Begum also believed in the people of Bhopal and trusted that they would work even if paid less. Qudsia Begum even gave Sikandar Jahan the command of her own army, which was quite expensive to maintain in those days (the expenditure of its upkeep was about Rs. 20,000).[9]

At this point, the Bhopal army showed signs of revolt. They were willing to take money from the Begums' enemies, Dastgir Mohammad Khan and Nawab Muiz Mohammad Khan, who had offered money to the army to gain support and wanted to overthrow Begum Sikandar Jahan. On 4 August, the mutineers planted two flags, *Nishan e Mohammadi* and *Nishan e Mahaviri*, to show their revolt. At the same time, Fazil Mohammad Khan and Adil Mohammad

Khan had sent a messenger to Bhopal to win over the soldiers of Bhopal contingent. There were also reports of Sepoys leaving State services and gathering at Rahatgarh to join Adil Mohammad Khan.

Dulhan Sahib, who was at Jehangirabad, advised Sikandar Jahan Begum to change the guards of the gates (main entrance to Bhopal city) to ensure more protection for the city. Dulhan Sahib and Balthazar Bourbon's son, Sebastian, made many of his Christian relatives the guardians of the gate because they were trusted and loyal. Sebastian was appointed Commander of the force in 1849. Sikandar Jahan Begum had asked him to control the internal rebellion of the Gonds and their allies. According to Saksena (1941), Sebastian Bourbon was seriously wounded in these battles.

Nawab Sikandar Jahan ordered five Muslims and five Hindus to bring back the flags of the mutineers. Majid Mohammad Khan had asked for a 12-day leave on 1 September 1857. Since he joined the mutineers, Nawab Sikandar Jahan Begum issued orders and instructions to Dulhan Sahib regarding the arrest of Zain ul Abidin, *Thanedar* of Ichhawar, as he was suspected of nefarious activities.[10] All this time, Sikandar Jahan Begum kept an eye on both the mutineers and the loyalist groups of the army and tackled them thoughtfully. Though she was under pressure from the Political Agent to act stringently against mutineers in the army, she preferred to deal with them without violence. Nawab Sikandar Jahan also issued orders to recruit fresh *jawan*s (soldiers) from the Bhopal contingent who were willing to serve the British. Munshi Bhawani Prasad reported that, as per the orders of the Nawab, a list was being prepared of the mutinous Sepoys, and 59 names had already been noted. After Murawwat Mohammad Khan forwarded the list, Nawab Sikandar Jahan Begum announced the dismissal of 137 sepoys of the contingent.

The British were contemplating the disbandment of the 77th Battalion of the Bhopal Army, since many were joining Fazil Mohammad Khan. Nawab Sikandar Jahan requested that Nawab Qudsia Begum stop the people of Bari from going to Rahat Garh to join Fazil Mohammad Khan. Bari came under Nawab Qudsia Begum's jurisdiction. Qudsia replied that the unemployed in Bari could not be stopped from joining the services of Fazil Mohammad Khan. Raja Mardan Sahi also communicated that five foreigners resigned from his services, mainly due to the demand to increase their pay.

Lord Canning appreciated Nawab Sikandar Jahan Begum's efforts. She ordered a phased dismissal of 59 soldiers of the army, as per Munshi Bhawani Prasad's list. They were paid their salary for the month of August. Wali Shah was one of the soldiers who was dismissed. It is interesting to note that 200 copies of the *ishtahar* (advertisement) were printed in Sikandari press declaring the arrest of the elephant of Fazil Mohammad Khan. At this point, the Bhopal State army was once again showing signs of revolt. This time they demanded many things, including two months' salary and *zarlain* (a tax that was deducted from their salary for the construction of the houses for the soldiers). Adil Mohammad Khan tried to incite Muslim soldiers for *jihad*. To pacify them, the Nawab distributed money to one of the contingents.

Maharani Lakshmi Bai of Jhansi was also putting pressure on Nawab Sikandar Jahan Begum to fight against the British. Lakshmi Bai wrote to the Nawab saying, 'I will attack Bhopal with a spear.' Sikandar Jahan Begum wrote back that 'Bhopal is always with the British and for you also, there are guns ready to welcome you.'[11] At this time, Nawab Sikandar Jahan Begum's only adviser was Nawab Baqi Mohammad Khan, as Jamal Uddin Khan Madar ul Maham was traveling to Mecca for the Haj. Fazil Mohammad Khan and Adil Mohammad Khan were increasing their influence and forces. After consultations with her officers, the Nawab decided to act decisively; she removed the troublesome officers from their state posts. In November 1857, Nawab Sikandar Jahan Begum issued orders to arrest or expel them from the state. The Nawab ordered the siege of the Garhi, their hiding place, as suggested by the British political agent. The Bhopal Commander of the forces did not support this decision, but the Nawab insisted on it. Munshi Husain Khan, private adviser to Naab Sikandar Jahan Behum, reported the progress of the seige of Garhi Ambapani. Nawab Sikandar Jahan Begum issued orders to chase and kill Fazil Mohammad Khan, Adil Mohammad Khan, and Aqil Mohammad Khan. On 25 November, Nawab Sikandar Jahan Begum was informed that Rahat Garh Fort had been vacated by the rebels.

In December, the army of Fazil Mohammad Khan, consisting of 2,000 men, surrendered at Rahat Garh Fort, marched from Jaisi Nagar to Sheikhpur and Dhilawar, and camped at Tendu Kheri. Sikandar Jahan Begum's trusted *risala*s of Sikh Sawars were deployed against the forces of Fazil Mohammad Khan. On 1 January, the contingent left for Sehore reluctantly, as they had doubts about their safety. They argued that they were the Begum's employees and had no concern with the English. However, on the Begum's assurance, they complied with her orders. General Hughes arrived in Sehore with his forces on 16 January 1858. Medical officer Thomas Lowe was with him. They were welcomed in Bhopal and met Sikandar Jahan Begum and Shahjahan Begum. Thomas Lowe later wrote in *Central India During the Rebellion of 1857-58* of the many episodes about his journey and the conditions of Bhopal. He wrote that on arriving in Ashta they heard that there was a big force of mutineers in Sehore and the Bhopal Contingent were awaiting their arrival. They were welcomed by a force of Bhopal in Ashta. On the way management was good and the countryside was beautiful. They arrived in Sehore on 15 January 1858. The Bhopal contingent was in a better condition and the faithful soldiers were treated accordingly.

Most of the soldiers who were faithful were Sheikhs. Many of the mutineers were under protection. A trial court was formed in the beginning of January; 149 soldiers of the Bhopal contingent were found guilty and orders were to shoot them down. Sikandar Jahan Begum established a liaison with the rebels and tried to pacify them. The rebels replied that they were with the Begum, but not with the British.

On 24 January, Rahat Garh was attacked, and after three days it was captured. Fazil Mohammad Khan tried to escape and hid in the bushes, but he was captured. Mardan Singh, Raja Banpur of District Sagar, tried his best to save the fort by mounting an attack, but ultimately got captured. Adil Mohammad Khan escaped with no trace. On 26 January 1858 (10 Jamadi us Sani) and the following days, the English started artillery fire on Rahat Garh Fort and captured the *burj* (highest point). In this process, five British soldiers were injured. On 1 July 1858, Sikandar Jahan Begum declared that peace was restored in the state. *The Illustrated London News* dated 16 May 1863, was filled with praise for Nawab Sikandar Begum.

The Aftermath of the Mutiny of 1857

As the British recovered control, Her Majesty the Queen of England communicated that the support given by Nawab Sikandar Begum during the crisis was ultimate proof of Bhopal's loyalty to the British government and had earned the Queen's lasting gratitude. It is said that when a close confidant of Sikandar Begum asked her what she would have done if the British had lost, she replied, 'In that event, the Bhopal army had made sure that the British garrison was neutralized!' Sikandar Begum had ensured that; by surrounding the British garrison in Sehore she had set up a situation where she would win even if the British had been overthrown in the uprising. After the uprising, the British government took over from the East India Company and ruled India directly and formally as a colony.

In 1861, Sikandar Jahan Begum awarded *jagir*s and medals to supporters who helped her during the mutiny, including Dulhan Sahib. Sebastian had displayed outstanding loyalty and leadership of the Bhopal army. He fought many battles for Sikandar Begum. He was seriously wounded when she sent him to command the forces against a few relatives who had joined hands with the Gond tribe to plan a conspiracy against the Begum (Kincaid 1887).

Conclusion

The Bourbons had helped the Begums to rule Bhopal State for two centuries. The Bourbons and the Begums began their loyal relationship with Manji Mamola (1728–95) when Salvador de Bourbon, alias Inayat Masih, came to Bhopal in 1785. This period was followed by the reign of Qudsia Begum (1819–1837) with the help of Balthazar Bourbon, alias Shahzad Masih. The next ruler of Bhopal was Nawab Sikandar Begum (1844–1868), who ruled with help from Sebastian Bourbon, the adopted son of Balthazar Bourbon and Dulhan Sahib. Sebastian continued his service during the region of Shahjahan Begum (1868–1901). (Refer to Appendix I: Bhopal's Rulers and the Bourbons for more details). According to the historian William Kincaid, the Bourbons were 'the most influential and wealthiest family in Bhopal, only after the Royal family themselves' (Kincaid 1887, 164).

Endnotes

1. Gazetteer Bhopal State, *Asiatic Quarterly Review*, 1857, p. 107; Kinçaid (1887).

2. Inayat Masih 514/1, Sanad and Jagir papers.

3. Letter in *Times of India*, 1 August 1857.

4. Alias Babar Masih, Dominick Bourbon was the son of Francis II, alias Sosher Bourbon. Dominick Bourbon was a first cousin of Salvador Bourbon (i.e. Balthazar Bourbon's uncle).

5. *Hayat Sikandari* by Sultan Jahan Begum, p.40-41, National Archives of Bhopal.

6. According to the account of a British lady, recorded in Indian Office Library Records.

7. Mutiny papers descriptive list, Vol I, NAI Bhopal, pp. 14-5, File no. 4, pp. 3-27.

8. Extract from *Gazetteer of India*, Bhopal State, Volume 3 Compiled by Capt. C. F. Luard, Ichhawar was given to Bhopal State under the Treaty of 1818. Also *Bengal Past and Present* Vol. XXV, Parts 1 and 2, January—June 1923).

9. *Hayat-i-Qudsi* by Sultan Jahan Begum, 1917, p. 144

10. Mutiny Papers descriptive list Vol. IV, NAI Bhopal, p. 48, File no. 1, p. 81.

11. *Tazkira-e-Baqi* (Life of Nawab Baqi Mohammad Khan) by Sultan Jahan Begum, Matba Sultani, 1915, p. 58.

THE FRENCH ARCHITECTURAL INFLUENCE IN BHOPAL

Shaukat Mahal, the palace of the Bourbons
Source: Abdul Mujeeb Faruqui, *Hindustan Times*, 22 April 2015

Shaukat Mahal, the palace of the Bourbons was in the news in 2015. The accompanying photograph is of the façade of Shaukat Mahal, which had developed deep cracks. The palace is said to be 180 years old. The palace was crumbling, as there has been no upkeep of this historic building.[1] The once-upon-a-time palace of the Bourbons has been a witness of Bhopal's

history for more than a century. It is now surrounded by busy roads and still houses 21 families, but was in shambles with no one taking care of this heritage building. Due to its crumbling parts, the building was declared unsafe to reside in and was also seen as a threat to the busy road below it. Press photographer Abdul Mujeeb Farooqui was among the people who saw this beautiful historical marvel collapse. Along with the fallen façade of the palace the history of the Bourbons was also lost.

Bhopal Municipal Corporation (BMC) had inspected 900 old structures in Bhopal, out of which 75 were declared in a dilapidated condition and 'unfit for human habitation'.[2] The BMC thus decided to bring down the building. In July 2015, Shaukat Mahal's 45-feet-high crown was brought down despite multiple protests by heritage lovers, including Susheila Ghosal (of the Bourbon family). Archaeologists still believed that the heritage site could have been saved.

Going back to the 19th century, the Bourbon Prime Ministers left a distinct mark on the buildings they constructed in Bhopal. The French-influenced

Demolition of Shaukat Mahal, the palace of the Bourbons Source: Abdul Mujeeb Faruqui, *Hindustan Times*, 12 July 2015

A photographer captures the demolition of Shaukat Mahal, the palace of the Bourbons
Source: Abdul Mujeeb Faruqui, *Hindustan Times*, 12 July 2015

architecture of these buildings is noteworthy. The minarets with typical French engraving are a proof of this Indo-French amalgamation. 'Shaukat Mahal' or the Grand Palace of Bhopal is situated at the heart of the city known as Iqbal Maidan or previously called the Khirni wala Maidan. The history of Shaukat Mahal dates back to 1817.[3] At that time only Manji ki Haveli (Manji Mamola's palace) existed. Nazar Mohammad Khan had built a palace for his newly wedded wife, Qudsia Begum. The palace was initially named Gauhar Mahal as Qudsia's original name was Gauhar Ara Begum. Her name was later changed to Qudsia Begum (Qudsia means holy). Since Nazar Mohammad was very close to his friend and minister Shahzad Masih he ordered the construction of the palace of Shahzad Masih (Shahzad Masih ki Haveli). Near Shahzad Masih ki Haveli was another palace built for Jahangir Muhammad Khan by Qudsia Begum around 1827 as he was a teenager at that time. This

palace was actually built for Amir Muhammad Khan who was the elder brother of Jahangir Muhammad Khan. Amir was originally chosen to marry Sikandar Begum, the prospective ruler of Bhopal. Later, this palace was further extended by Jahangir Muhammad Khan and the palace of Shahzad Masih was merged into it and together it was called Shaukat Mahal.

Left: Entrance of Gauhar Mahal, palace of Qudsia Begum

Right: Inside view of Gauhar Mahal, Bhopal
Source: Author's private collection

In 1844 when Jahangir died, Sikandar Begum came back to Shaukat Mahal, started residing here and began the construction of Moti Mahal. There is a tunnel leading to the lake, with a small gate near Gauhar Mahal. In those days, it was meant to be an escape route in case of emergency. At present it is used as a sewage line running from Shaukat Mahal (previously called Shahzad Masih ki Haveli) to the rear entrance of Gauhar Mahal. Shaukat Mahal is internally connected with Sultan Manzil, the residence

The tunnel entrance seen by the stairs and the rear gate of Gauhar Mahal leading to the Shaukat Mahal
Source: Author's private collection

of Sultan Jahan Begum, and Hamid Manzil where Nawab Hamidullah Khan was born.

After the demise of Shahzad Masih, his wife, Madam Dulhan continued to reside in the women's wing (Zeenat Mahal) of the palace. During this time Sebastian Bourbon continued to make architectural improvements to the palace by constructing front portions and some modifications in the inner area especially of Zeenat Mahal, the ladies wing. These changes and additions showed more signs of the French architectural influence.

Since Shaukat Mahal was first built for Shahzad Masih as his *haveli* or palace, it is quite different in architecture from the rest of the structures in the city. For instance, usually Muslim architecture has semicircular niches or *mihrab* that have only one central corner. This palace has two corners in these semicircular niches. The palace has a charming combination of Gothic and post-Renaissance styles. The unique feature of the palace is the beautiful alabaster-white building having a series of intricate triangular-shaped arches on its roof. The exterior of the palace has exquisite floral patterned carvings of the fleur-de-lis, which is a French symbol that shows the motif of a lily with three of its petals joined together near the base.

Bottom: Inner view of the gate of Shaukat Mahal

Extreme bottom: Fleur-de-lis pattern on the gate of Shaukat Mahal
Source: Author's private collection

The difference in the minarets of Moti Mahal and Shaukat Mahal

Front view of Shaukat Mahal before demolition
Source: Author's private collection

are quite stark. The arches are a bit different in their formation. Many historic buildings in Bhopal have a blend of Islamic and Gond styles but Shaukat Mahal has a distinct Indo-European style of architecture. Shaukat Mahal's main gate is decorated with blue floral paintings. It is about 26 feet high so that an elephant can easily pass through it. Shaukat Mahal is a three-tier building. The door is wooden with iron nails on it so that it cannot be broken by a charging elephant in case of an attack. These doors are very heavy but at the same time they can be shut with little effort. These doors still stand tall in present-day Bhopal. There are two Mughal style arches at the main entrance, the inner one has the floral design of fleur-de-lis. As we enter the main gate we can see the courtyard that is big enough for a carriage.

All around the courtyard is a two-level structure. The upper level has large windows for the sunlight to come in. These large windows have French style arches. The railing of the roof is decorated with

Inner courtyard of Shaukat Mahal
Source: Author's private collection

fine French motifs. The *jaali* or the latticed screen inside the palace is made of cast iron. This screens the corridors of Sawan Bhadon, which is a perennial water fountain situated in the middle of the palace. *Sawan* and *Bhadon* are the names of the months of the monsoon season according to the Hindu calendar. These months are associated with romance and love. Numerous poems and songs have been written on these months celebrating the mood of this romantic season. The Bourbons and Begums used the rainwater to devise a natural cooling system inside the palace. The quadrangle in Shaukat Mahal known as Sawan Bhadon has nozzles near the ceilings through which water percolated to air cool the palace. In the middle of the courtyard stands a highly ornamented fountain made of brass and copper. There is a common saying that this fountain is perennial with the Bhopal Lake as the feeder. The railing of the Sawan Bhadon is ornamented with the French symbol, i.e. fleur-de-lis. Right round the fountain there is a two-tier building. On every floor there is a water system that flows through small holes, with drops of moisture falling on the floor beneath, thus giving an illusion of rain

Top: Carved arches of Shaukat Mahal

Bottom: Double pointed niches on windows in Shaukat Mahal
Source: Author's private collection

and at the same time cooling the structure. The view of the Sawan Bhadon with the water tank is still present in Bhopal.

The roof was a very important portion of any building in those days, as it provided fresh air and people used to sit there in the evening to socialize and for entertainment. The walls of the roof are high to provide privacy to the ladies. Another reason was *purdah* or the custom of keeping women hidden from the sight of outsiders, due to which the walls of the roof must be of a certain height.

As we enter into the gallery joining Shaukat Mahal to Zeenat Mahal, the ladies wing, we get the impression of entering a grand palace with the light filtering in.

Top: Corridor in Shaukat Mahal

Top right: Long distance view from above and close-up view of Sawan Bhadon in Shaukat Mahal
Source: Author's private collection

Zeenat Mahal is constructed in such a way that most of it can be seen from the outside. This is the Palace where Madame Dulhan and Sebastian Bourbon used to live. The palace has a unique French architecture. However, the main gate has the typical Mughal arch. Since Zeenat Mahal was the ladies wing among the palaces it has a smaller entrance. The main gate has two levels above it. The gate is decorated with the motif of the fleur-de-lis in the centre and the pattern continues on both sides. There are four windows on either side of the gate while on its inner side there are nine windows. Above the gate on the third floor there are five windows while the middle one is elongated in width with three small partitions. There is also a railing in front of these windows on the second floor. The arches of the windows depict a typical Mughal style of architecture. The crown of the gate has seven quadrangle windows and two minarets and two small conical shaped decorations.

On the western side of the gate, i.e. towards Shaukat Mahal, there are five windows each, on all the three floors. The palace also has coloured window panes which was a very new technique in those days. The designs on the arches are in French style. The patterns of these arches are symmetric and different from each other. For example, on the top floor the outer two arches on the windows are similar and in triangular form. The next two arches on the inner side of these arches are similar but different from the outer ones. They are semicircular but pointed. The middle one is totally different from the others. The same pattern is followed in the arches of the other floors. In front is a railing with the fleur-de-lis pattern but in the middle it is pointed like a javelin. This railing covers the entire front of the Zeenat Mahal.

Front view of Zeenat Mahal, near Shaukat Mahal

Bottom: Railing with fleur-de-lis pattern at Zeenat Mahal
Source: Author's private collection

Rear view of Shaukat Mahal, showing the church steeple Source: Author's private collection

The rear side of Shaukat Mahal has a chapel-like structure with a tower. This church-like structure is at the top floor of Shaukat Mahal. The stairs leading to the chapel are connected to a hall and open verandah. Above the verandah is the tower which is triangular in shape. The structure resembles a prayer room for Christians. Since Balthazar Bourbon and his family resided in the palace and he was a devout Christian, it is reasonable to assume that the family must have had a prayer room. It appears that the tower had a bell, or a statue, probably of St. Francis Xavier, their patron saint. The Church in Jehangirabad was also named after him. Probably later this bell or statue was removed. The Christian Church in the middle of Bhopal city shows the liberal atmosphere of the ruling Muslim community. It is believed that Salvador and Balthazar Bourbon were both staunch Christians. This is evident from a few instances, such as, before going to guard the *Tazia*, Balthazar first went to the chapel to pray, as told by Magdaline Bourbon. The family followed all the Christian prayer rituals. Even in Dulhan Sahib Mahal there was a chapel. A priest performed the prayers for the family and was given a stipend by the Bourbons. In the Catholic Church in Jehangirabad there was a dedicated space for the Bourbons.

Close-up view of the church steeple at Shaukat Mahal Source: Author's private collection

It is very unfortunate that due to rapid urbanization and lack of maintenance, Shaukat Mahal has lost its glory. With its collapse, Bhopal has lost a unique architectural marvel that was a beacon of Indo-French culture and architecture.

Endnotes

1. Sravani Sarkar, 'Bhopal's 180-year-old architectural marvel Shaukat Mahal in a shambles,' *Hindustan Times*, April 22, 2015,

http://www.hindustantimes.com/bhopal/bhopal-s-180-year-old-architectural-marvel-shaukat-mahal-in-a-shambles/story-0HY8Il3cxE2JBCKJ5yUKmK.html

2. HT Correspondent, 'Bhopal civic body pulls down Shaukat Mahal's crown,' *Hindustan Times*, July 12, 2015,

http://www.hindustantimes.com/bhopal/bhopal-over-75-old-unfit-structures-to-face-civic-body-s-hammer/story RB93Ox9WzOhNjrw0GIS08L.html

3. Adapted from Rizwan uddin Ansari's version of the history of Shaukat Mahal (https://www.youtube.com/watch?v=QwjMqMHk7mw).

THE LEGACIES OF *GANGA-JAMUNI TEHZEEB* AND BRAVE LADIES IN BHOPAL

Ganga-Jamuni tehzeeb is the term used to describe the unique cultural fusion that arose when Hindus and Muslims lived together in the central plains of Northern India. The term probably came into existence in the medieval period, when the region was called Awadh. A long history of *Ganga-Jamuni tehzeeb* has given Bhopal a culture that is distinct in many ways. People of different religions live in harmony by imbibing other cultures and traditions around them.

The Distinct Cultural Fusion of Bhopal

Under the rule of Muslim Begums in Bhopal, Hindus and Muslims alike were cared for by the State. Hindu festivals were encouraged and the Begums themselves participated. Intermingling in Bhopal brought about a very unique blend of customs and rituals. In those days, people used to sit on *patia*s, resting places in most communities, where folks came together to discuss the day's events. People spent evenings discussing politics, local happenings, and cultural events, and even played chess and *chousar* (a traditional Indian game). Crowds used to gather near the Jumerati, Atta Shuja Khan, Jehangirabad, and Shahjahanabad areas of Bhopal. Even now, the *patia*s near Moti Mahal, just in front of Shaukat Mahal, remain busy with both the young and the old; the most common pastime is playing chess.

A mushaira (Urdu poetry recitation session) at Iqbal Maidan, in front of Zeenat Mahal and Shaukat Mahal Source: Author's private collection

My mother, Magdaline Bourbon, often spoke about her life in the palace (Shaukat Mahal), and at the Bourbon Palace (known as Dulhan Sahib ka Mahal) at Lakherapura, built by the Bourbons. As a young girl, Magdaline often visited Sultan Jahan Begum at Qasre Sultani or Ahmadabad Palace, and had many interesting stories about life at the Begum's Palace. For the Hindu festival of Holi (also called the festival of colours), all the Hindu ladies were called from the city to the palace. A large tank would be filled with water and *tesu* flowers (also called *palash* or *Butea monosperma*) were put in the tank to give it a natural orange colour. Muslim women also played Holi at the palace. New clothes were given to all the guests for their return home. Sweets and dried fruits were kept in big *thal*s (trays). Women singers were called for entertainment. On one occasion, the Begum liked the song so much that she threw silver and gold coins to the singer. A few of the gold coins landed on my mother, but she quickly threw them towards the singer. Sultan Jahan Begum noticed this and appreciated my mother's honest gesture.

For every festival, my mother was invited to the palace. During the Muslim Eid festival at Chowk

Bazaar, Bhopal's main market in those days, Hindus used to spread cloth for Muslims to pray during *Jumatul vida* (the last Friday of Ramadan and Eid). Irrespective of caste or religion, everyone mingled in a very integrated way. Even during the India–Pakistan Partition riots in 1947, Bhopal was probably the only Muslim state in India that had no communal turmoil. In 1947 during Hindu–Muslim riots, many people travelling in trains were killed trying to cross the Indian border. It is said that Nawab Hamidullah Khan ordered the blood-stained trains to be washed before they arrived in, or passed through, Bhopal. This was done to avoid disturbing the comparative peace of the city. Nawab Hamidullah Khan was very mindful about maintaining the multicultural characteristics of Bhopal. One day, when a Hindu's betel nut shop was brought down by some miscreants, Nawab Hamidullah Khan himself visited that place and ordered strict action against the perpetrator. He also awarded a small compensation to the shop owner.

Bhopal's Women's Bazaar

During the reign of the Begums, Bhopal's Meena Bazaar, which was strictly for women, was a strongly guarded rectangle surrounded by shops. Known also as Pari Bazaar, which literally means market of the fairies, it still exists near All Saints School and the old MLA quarters. Sultan Jahan Begum, who had given the orders to construct Meena Bazaar, would arrive with her friends dressed in brightly coloured traditional Bhopali *churidar pyjama*s or leggings worn under long *kurta*s gathered at the waist and hanging down like a frock. This attire was worn with contrasting colour pleated *dupattas* (long scarves) of about four yards. The air was charged with the intoxicating smell of *ittar* (perfumed oils), accompanied by the soft tinkling of glass bangles.

The merchandise was sold by lower-middle class women, who were encouraged by the Nawab Begum to put up stalls to sell accessories to expand their household income. The Begums and other members of the royal family often visited the bazaar and made numerous purchases. Prices were never fixed, but depended on the generosity of fair clientele, with a view to help needy stall owners. The prices were treated as incentives for the deserving, and were conferred by the Nawab Begum when her retinue visited each stall. The Begums would favour sellers with a smile here or there, and sometimes picked up a new accessory as a gesture of appreciation. Sultan Jehan Begum once went to buy bangles, and the *chudiwali* (bangle seller) caught her hand and started layering bangles onto her wrist. When the *chudiwali* had completed this mission, she asked an exorbitant price. The Begum got annoyed and told her firmly that she would not be overcharged. The woman replied softly, 'I am not asking this price for the bangles, but for the price of the hands that wear the bangles'. The Begum smiled and handed this woman the full sum of money.

During the Mughal era, Meena Bazaars, known also as *Kuhs Ruz* (Days of Joy) were held by the elite women of Bhopal for each other. This tradition had started during Emperor Humayun's time. Later, Akbar and his successors made these events more elaborate. The fair was closed to the general public, while the women of the harem, Rajput ladies, and the wives and daughters of noblemen in the court set up their own stalls to sell cloth, jewellery, handicrafts, etc. The only males permitted to enter the bazaar were the emperor, princes, and some nobles, who purchased the goods, which were sold at high prices.

Another unique feature of Meena Bazaar was its raised platform, which was a popular meeting spot for groups of ladies. The elders exchanged gossip and discussed scandals, and the younger lot shared their romantic episodes and showed off recent perfume or fashion purchases. It is extremely sad that these wonderful heart-throbbing tales are a thing of the past for this historic space. The building still stands, sheltering a few unappealing government offices. Even now, though, under full moonlight when the atmosphere is calm, a ruffle of silk and subdued laughter rises and softly vanishes.

There is a famous story of a very beautiful and talented singer from the Delhi Court, who had come to Bhopal to show her talent. She quoted a fabulous amount that the Bhopali *jagirdar*s and *zamindar*s (landlords) could not afford. The singer chided them in the open marketplace, laughing that Bhopal could not afford a distinguished singer. One day, she was asked to perform at Shahjahan Begum's court. The moment she began singing the Begum shut her ears with her palms and loudly insisted that this untrained voice stop at once. The singer was duly paid the full amount, but after the insult she could not utter one word and went crying out of the *Durbar*. The much-amused courtiers got their revenge without uttering one word themselves.

The Legacy of Bhopal's Brave Ladies

My mother used to say there is something in the water of the Bhopal lake that makes the women of Bhopal very brave. My mother spoke often of Rani Kamlapati and her fierce strength. Rani Kamlapati was the daughter of Chaudhri Kirpa Ramchandar, and was married to Nizam Shah, the warlord of a Gond tribe. My mother told us that at that time only Bhils and Gonds lived near Bhopal Lake. The tribes of Malwa were constantly warring with each other. Rani Kamlapati was among the most beautiful and intelligent women of her time. It is said that she was so fair-skinned that when she used to have a paan (betel nut leaf), one could see the colour trickling down her throat. She was considered the power behind her husband. With her as his queen, Nizam Shah was very successful, until he was poisoned by his rival, Alam Shah, of Chainpur-Bara. Rani Kamlapati sent a messenger to Dost Mohammad Khan, an Afghan warrior and the Nawab of Bhopal. The messenger carried one lakh rupees, and a *rakhi* (a sacred thread that symbolizes the relationship between a brother and sister in the Hindu tradition). This gesture to make the Nawab her brother came with a request that he kill Gond Raja, Alam Shah, of Chainpur-Bara, who had killed her husband. Dost kept his word and killed the Gond Raja. Afterwards, they say that Rani

Kamlapati took all her gold and jewels and drowned herself in the lake. She died in 1723. Today, of the seven levels of Kamlapati Mahal, two are submerged. Young boys still dive deep in search of the treasure in the lake.

When we used to pass Bhopal Lake, my mother almost always recited these lines:

Tal to Bhopal Tal aur sab talaiyya,
Rani to Kamlapati aur sab ranaiya,
Garh to Chitorgarh aur sab garhiya,
Raja to Ramchandra aur sub Rajaiya.

The first two lines mean that if there is a lake worth mentioning, it is Bhopal Lake; the rest are very small compared to it. Similarly, if there is a queen worth mentioning, she is Queen Kamlapati; the rest are not even worth mentioning.

It was only after Raja Bhoj of the Parmara dynasty that Bhopal State was cleared of its thick forest and built up. Rani Shyamli, alias Shamli (wife of Uday Verman Parmar, Raja of Dhar), can be considered the founder of Bhopal.[1] The elders often spoke about an education center in Chowk, in the middle of the city. The first education center was established in the old fort of Bhopal, at Shyamla Hills. Named after her, the fort was founded by Rani Salmali. It was a huge structure that took 23 years to complete and could be compared to Nalanda University. In 1220, it was situated in the area where Jama Masjid Bhopal now stands. In this school, the pundits taught the Vedas, Shastras, and other Hindu religious texts to

Top: Chota Talab, made by Chote Khan

Middle: A bridge known as Pul Pukta, Bhopal

Bottom: Rani Kamlapati's Palace, Bhopal Source: Author's private collection

more than 500 students. This institution lasted about 112 years, under Parmara protection.

The tradition of female leadership continued even with Dost Mohammad Khan, the first Nawab of Bhopal. Begum Fateh Bibi, wife of Dost Mohammad Khan, was his constant companion. She even accompanied him riding and shooting. One day, when Dost and Fateh Bibi were visiting an area near Bhopal, they became tired and decided to rest for the night. Fateh

Bibi dreamt that a *pir* (a saint) advised her that she needed to build a fort at that exact location. She told her husband about this dream. Dost agreed, and that was the beginning of Fatehgarh Fort in 1722. Dost

Fatehgarh Fort or Bhopal Fort
Source: Author's private collection

and Fateh Bibi were the builders of the early Bhopal State. Later, the the fort was named after Fateh Bibi.[2]

In the early years, it was next to impossible for women to rule in a Muslim Pathan state, yet it became possible in Bhopal. The first woman ruler of Bhopal state was Manji Mamola Bi (1715–1795). She ruled for many years (from 1728 to 1795), along with Yar Mohammad Khan. She was the power behind her two step-sons, Faiz Mohammad Khan and Hayat Mohammad Khan. Being a Hindu woman, she gained respect from both Muslims and Hindus. Until as recently as the 19th century, Bhopal and the surrounding areas were inhabited primarily by Hindus. Manji Mamola Bi or Mamola Begum ruled for 50 years, until she was 80 years old. She is said to have had a keen political and administrative acumen. She realized the fast-growing influence of the British and was the first to offer a hand of friendship. When Salvador Bourbon arrived in Bhopal in 1783, seeing a Frenchman speaking good English, Mamola Begum decided to offer him land and a position in the Bhopal State army.

Another of the many stories my mother used to narrate was about Balthazar Bourbon's *Tazia* incident. Salvador's son, Balthazar Bourbon, used to take the *Tazia* (a religious procession) to Karbala. The Shia sect of Muslims took *Tazia*s every year, as a symbol of the tombs of Imam Husain and his associates who were slaughtered in Karbala during the seventh century AD. In addition, they took *Alam*, the flag of Imam Husain and his relatives. Although Balthazar was a Christian, he followed Shia customs. Since he was very close to the Begum, he had many enemies. He and Qudsia Begum came to know of a plot to assassinate him during the *Tazia* procession. She warned him not to participate, as there was a threat to his life. But Balthazar was a brave man and refused to listen. He instructed his son, Sebastian, to kill every Bourbon lady as soon as he heard of Balthazar's death. This was to avoid the Bourbon women being ill-treated by the Pathans. The ladies were ready for this eventuality. Along with Dulhan Sahib, Balthazar's mother, they sat in one room, prepared, praying for Balthazar. When they heard he was safe, they all sighed with shared relief. The fact that none of them tried to flee showed their incredible courage and loyalty.

Dulhan Sahib was considered the leader of about 500 Christian families after Balthazar's death. The royal family sought Dulhan Sahib's advice on many matters. As mentioned, in *Hayat-i-Qudsi*, Nawab Jahangir Muhammad Khan, husband of Sikandar Begum, was once surrounded in Astha Fort. His mother-in-law Qudsia Begum sent Sikandar Begum and Dulhan Sahib with some state officials to get the Nawab back. They stayed for about 24 hours and then returned with the Nawab. To this day, the women of Bhopal are fiercely independent.

As described in a previous chapter, during the famous seige of Bhopal in 1812, it was cut off from other states for six months. The women of Bhopal played a major role in defending Bhopal State from the Marathas. The pivotal battle was led by Zeenat Begum, mother of Qudsia Begum. Hindu and Muslim ladies took off their veils and joined the army. They supplied water and food to the soldiers. They even filled gunpowder in the cannons. After many months of battle, the Wazir decided to fight this last battle with few soldiers. It was a lost battle since the opponent could easily defeat a few men. The women decided to wear men's attire to deceptively portray the army as having a huge contingent. They all stood on the walls to show the Marathas that Bhopal had enough men to fight. Surprisingly, the enemies withdrew and Bhopal was saved.

The Begums led Bhopal toward its preeminent status as a wonderful multicultural city. This continued until the last of their rule, with Maimoona Sultan. Maimoona Sultan, wife of then Nawab Hamidullah

Khan, was a gracious lady. She was extremely beautiful and very well mannered. She could converse on any topic. Married at the age of five, she was especially groomed to rule. My own grandfather, Bipin Ghosal, a curator of the only museum in Central India, was appointed to teach her English. As soon as he used to arrive to teach the girls, the young Begum would scream and tell the others to observe *purdah*. She would say, *'Jaldi purdah karo purdah karo,'* which means 'hurry and cover your heads'. But the unusual part was she didn't follow the custom of *purdah* herself.

Begum Maimoona Sultan, wife of Nawab Hamidullah Khan, with Susheila Ghosal Source: Author's private collection

This is a photograph of my younger sister, Susheila Ghosal, meeting with Begum Maimoona Sultan. We used to visit her in the palace often. The maids would serve us tea or coffee. We used to find it very strange that the tray came with two small jugs instead of the customary one milk jug. The second jug contained melted sugar or molasses. The Begum informed us that this was done so that grains of sugar would not come into the mouth, and because the noise of stirring sugar in a teacup was too harsh.

The last of the queens of Nizam Shah's family were Rani Feroz Kunwar and Rani Mardan Kunwar. Rani Feroz Kunwar (1882–1932) is buried in Bara Bagh in Bhopal. She was the last Gond Ruler of Bari. In her time, she had a seal in her name with the inscription

'Mein Kundan Gondi, Rani Bari Infizal' (I am Gond Queen of Bari). She was so powerful that she had a strange tradition of putting a *tilak* (mark) on the forehead of men she appointed for her service. Instead of her fingers, she used her toe.

Bhopali women continue their tradition of bravery. My mother once saw a snake in the house when I was a very young girl. Without hesitation, she handed me a gun and ordered me to shoot the snake. There is no question that even today women in Bhopal are different from women in the rest of India. Women from Bhopal drive jeeps and compete in car rallies, but they also play a more traditional role and look after their families. Without a doubt, these women reflect a beautiful legacy of bravery.

Endnotes

1. Pratipal Bhatia, *The Paramaras,* c. 800–1305 AD (New Delhi: Munshiram Manoharlal Publishers, 1970), p. 15.

2. *Gazetteer Of India Madhya Pradesh, Bhopal State,* as cited in C. F. Luard, Captain, Superintendent Gazetteer in Central India, Central Agency, Indore, 15th September 1907.

CHAPTER 8

THE DECLINE OF THE BOURBONS IN BHOPAL

The Bourbon family had a history of being very dear to the Bhopal royal family. The Bourbons were very loyal towards the Begums and this relationship continued to grow stronger with each generation. In return, the royal family bestowed upon them gifts such as land and maintenance allowances for the up-keep of their families. In those times, the Bourbons were said to be 'the most influential and wealthiest family in Bhopal, only after the Royal family themselves' (Kincaid 1887). The Bhopal royal family gifted land to the Bourbons so they could settle down in Bhopal and subsequently honoured them with more land for their loyalty towards the royal family. In 1786 Salvador Bourbon (Inayat Masih) received a *jagir* of two villages and also funds to cover his expenses. Later on these *jagir*s were confiscated during the reign of Nawab Nazar Mohammad Khan (1816–1819). Thereafter, one *moza* (revenue estate), dadar Pargana Gulgaon, amounting to Rs. 15,000 was restored in the year 1822 in the name of Hakim

Shahzad Masih and his brother Philip Bourbon alias Imdad Masih (Kincaid 1887).

In the year 1822 another 21 *moza* were granted to Shahzad Masih and further in 1827 he was granted Rs 6,151 to meet the expenditure of the officers of service to the Bourbons. The funds were also used for the upkeep of elephants, horses and their riders, *palki* (palanquins to carry ladies in *purdah*), policemen and guards. In the same year another *taluqa* (revenue district) was awarded to him amounting to Rs. 41,900. Also a *Sanad* (legal document) was given to him, a right to have a freehold land, which could be passed on from generation to generation. In 1930, Shahzad Masih was awarded another area near Bhopal called Icchawar in exchange for a few villages. These land donations from the Bhopal royalty to the Bourbons got renewed from time to time. On 28 February 1838, Mr Elvis Sahab Bahadur, Political Agent of Bhopal, renewed these grants.

Upon Balthazar Bourbon or Hakim Shahzad Masih Sahib's death, the property was again confiscated in 1840 during the reign of Jahangir Muhammad Khan. At the same time there was a demand to recover the arrears amounting to Rs 41,900 from Dulhan Sahib which she was unable to pay. She pleaded to Wilkinson Sahib Bahadur who did not favour her. He wrote back saying that since the Nawab Sahib is not in her favour, therefore his hands are tied. Representatives of the department of Political Agents also tried to intervene in favour of Dulhan Sahib. They included Hakim Ghulam Husain

Sahab, Syed Gouhar Ali, Huzair Husain and Maulvi Haidar Nawaz. However, all this effort went in vain. After the Nawab Jahangir Muhammad Khan Sahib's death in 1254 Fasli, Nawab Sikandar Begum helped the Bourbon family. Later in 1848, after a request from Dulhan Sahib, Nawab Sikandar Jahan Begum restored the *jagir* of Rs 50,000. In the year 1851 a further 22 *moza* (revenue estate) amounting to Rs 54,000 was awarded to her. At the same time an agreement was signed with Bibi Sahiba, wife of Philip Bourbon, for the livelihood of the descendants of Philip Bourbon, the brother of Balthazar Bourbon (Shahzad Masih) in 1860. After the death of Bibi Sahiba, the political agent confiscated the property and in return allotted small grants. In the year 1883 the total *jagir* in the name of Dulhan Sahib amounted to Rs 86,430. This amount was used to take care of the guards of Garhi Ichhawar and management of *chowki*s (check posts), *pargana* (administrative subdivision larger than *tehsil* and smaller than *zilla*), officers and servants of *tehsil* (district administration), *thana* (police station) and post office, etc. However, this generosity towards the Bourbons was about to end.

Among the Bourbons, Dulhan Sahib, wife of Balthazar Bourbon, was the highest paid *Jagirdar*. She played the most important role of being a chieftain of the Bourbon clan as well for the Christian community in Bhopal. Qudsia Begum had given Madam Dulhan the charge of looking after the young Shahjahan Begum. She served as the 'lady in waiting' or person who is nearest to Qudsia Begum.

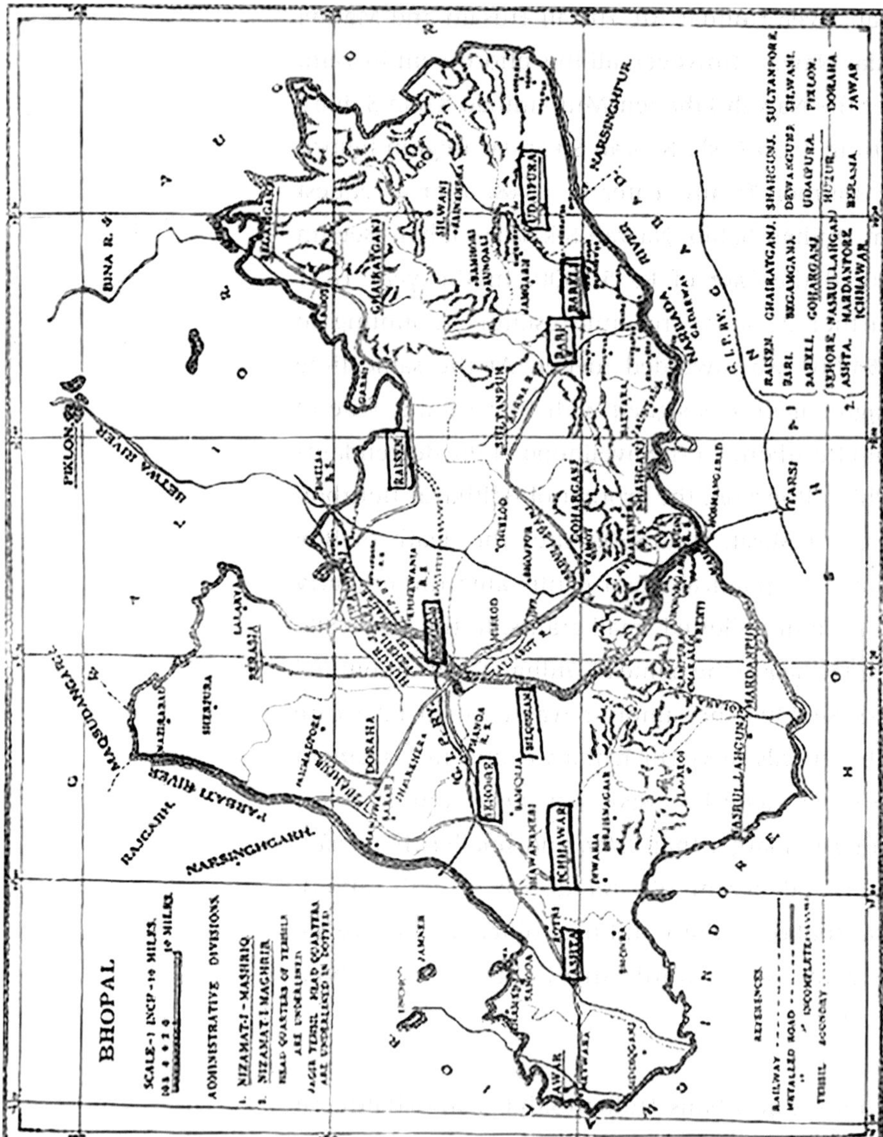

Map of Bhopal State showing the Bourbon properties as marked
Source: Author's private collection

The last of the Bourbons to receive largesse from the Royal family of Bhopal was Magdaline Ghosal née Bourbon, who owned 62 acres of land in the middle of Bhopal city, Jehangirabad, till late 1986. The Madhya Pradesh Government acquired 50 acres of that land to build police quarters at the rate of Rs 1,000 per acre. My mother continued to get her monthly payment of Rs 30/- as *mansab* (to cover monthly expenses) which she received from the Begums, till her death. Every year she used to go to the Government treasury to get her money. She was grateful to Nawab Hamidullah Khan for helping her to get her *mansab*.

Colonel Kincaid described the Bhopal Bourbons in these words, 'The latter history of family furnishes a sketch of Bhopal history for the last three quarters of a century. The fidelity of Bourbons is not more admirable than the generous acknowledgements and rewards bestowed upon them by the chiefs they served, were honorably acquired' (Kincaid 1887, 176). He further adds a few remarks with reference to the changes in the Bourbon family's customs and habits owing to the long settlement in India. He concludes that, 'Their circumstances, by the reduction of their landed property, since the death of Madame Dulhin, are not nearly so flourishing as they used to be' (ibid.). He explains that one the reasons could be that 'inter–marriage with individuals of oriental race, darken their complexion', which made the Bourbons lose their identity.

R.V. Smith in his writings in *The Hindu* mentions that Bhopal witnessed the end of the Zamindari system as well as the rift between the Royal family of the state and the Bourbons. This break-up triggered the decline of the Bourbons. He narrates that a few of the Bourbon clan managed to settle down abroad and one of their branches married into the Bengali Ghosal family.[1] The

Bengali family branch is where my mother belongs. After Indian Independence in 1947, Bhopal was rapidly changing. My mother often remembered the past, especially when she saw Bhopal's old buildings. She had very pleasant memories of the yacht club of Nawab Hamidullah Khan Sahib. She used to narrate stories of Nawab Sahib hunting the Siberian cranes. These Siberian cranes used to migrate to India to avoid the fierce winters up north in their native regions.

There are multiple conjectures to explain the decline of the Bourbons. One is that the people believed in allegations of the love affair between Qudsia Begum and Balthazar Bourbon, because of which the Royal family decided to part ways with the Bourbons. In 1829 jealous Afghan courtiers poisoned Balthazar. But the alleged love affair may not be true and even after Balthazar, the Bourbon descendants continued to be appointed by the ruling family as Prime Ministers of Bhopal State. The second conjecture is that when the Government of India in the early 1980s decided to take away the *jagir*s, this act also included confiscating the property owned by the Bourbons that ultimately resulted in making them commoners. In other cases, the Bourbons who had daughters had a natural eliminating process. Like my grandfather, Gasper Bourbon, whose only daughter Magdaline Bourbon married and later on settled outside the State in Gwalior and Agra.

There is no doubt that the Bourbons played a very significant role as advisers, guides and Prime Ministers assisting the royal family of Bhopal. There could be a combination of reasons for their loss of power which ultimately are just surmises at this point. Khan (2000) notes that the Bourbon's family fortune began to decline in the reign of Shahjahan Begum. It is said that Shahjahan Begum's second husband Siddiq Hassan was not secular and was not in favour of the Christian Bourbons' proximity with the royals. Khan (2000) narrates that the Bourbon *jagir*s were recovered by the Bhopal state. Khan further states that the stature of the Bourbons was not restored by subsequent Begums like Sultan Jahan even though she was considered to be religiously liberal. Though, Khan considers the reason for the Bourbon's decline to originate from the rumours about Qudsia Begum and Balthazar Bourbon.

There is another story that could be a potential reason for the decline of the Bourbons. Bonaventura Bourbon I died on 20 July 1894. Eight months after his father's death, the last son Bonaventura II alias Aijaz Masih was born on 31 March 1895. These dates are recorded at the Catholic Church of Jehangirabad, Bhopal. It was generally known that Bonventura I (Inayat Masih) had been ailing for a very long time before his death. Therefore, some people considered it unlikely for Bonaventura II, alias Aijaz Masih, to be born just eight months after his father's death. The Begum ruling Bhopal at that time was Shahjahan Begum (1868–1901) who was married to Sayyid Muhammad Hasan Khan. Both of them were orthodox, and were strict followers of the Muslim religion. Sultan Jahan Begum was a very pious lady, and observing this incident, decided to take away the *jagir*s from the Bourbons. After Bonaventura

Bourbon I died, his wife Veronica did not share a close affinity with the royal family. However, not all Bourbons were treated alike. Sultan Jahan Begum continued to give Magdaline Bourbon, my mother, her *mansab*. Magdaline Bourbon continued to live with the royal family, in Dulan Sahib ka Mahal, at Lakerapura.

The early Bourbons, with the exception of Jean Philippe and Juliana are buried in Agra in the old cemetery. As mentioned in Mesrovb Jacob Seth's book, *History of the Armenians in India, from the Earliest Times to the Present Day*, the Martyrose's Chapel is the oldest Christian edifice in Northern India. It was built in 1611 at the old Armenian Cemetery. Seth notes that one of the graves has the inscription of '162-1832-Bourbons, S, A., Mrs' (Seth 1897, 94) with the actual inscription in Armenian, since this is an Armenian cemetery. The author narrates that the tombs in this graveyard appear to be the descendants of John Philippe de Bourbon of Navarre. Mesrovb Jacob Seth notes that grave No. 162 is of Bibi Anna, daughter of Salvador Bourbon, alias Inayat Masih and wife of Pedro Bourbon (Imdad Masih). No. 163 is that of Pedro Bourbon, son of Khairat Masih. Their graves have a red stone monument built on a platform in a typical Mughal style. My mother, a devout Christian, used to light a candle each year on All Souls Day (02 November). The old cemetery is known as The Martyrose's Graveyard and is in front of the civil court. This is a centuries-old graveyard looked after by the Archaeological Department. Most graves have been erased, but since my mother knew the location of the graves, I was able to find the graves of the Bourbons. This is also where all the soldiers and English men of the time are buried. Agra's Armenian community is also buried there. They were brutally massacred by Aurangzeb in one small room 'Martyrose's Chapel' where they were praying.

The rest of the Bhopal Bourbons are buried in Bhopal. Balthazar Bourbon was also buried in his own garden in Bhopal. The Catholic register of Jehangirabad, Bhopal, records that there was a very old Christian graveyard on Besaria Road. The church records show that there were around 300 graves there. Many of the Bhopal Bourbons were also buried there. This includes graves of Bonaventura Bourbon II alias Aijaz Masih and his wife Philomena. The graveyard was Bourbons' landed property (*jagir*). After the Begums had taken away the *mansab*s and the *sanad*s from the Bourbons, the later generations of Bourbons were finding it hard to make their ends meet. One day, early in the morning, a tractor-trailer erased all the graves. A branch of the Bourbons sold the graveyard and hence none of the Bourbons graves can be found now. My mother Magdaline played no role in this since she was mainly living out of Bhopal with her husband. I am the only living witness to this property deal. The Bourbons who made this deal are all dead now and with them the history of the Bourbon graves in Bhopal has become lost in the mists of time.

Endnote

1. R.V. Smith, 'Balthazar's Bourbon bond,' *The Hindu*, March 12, 2007, Metro Plus, http://www.thehindu.com/todays-paper/tp-features/tp-metroplus/balthazars-bourbon-bond/article2242023.ece.

MAGDALINE BOURBON

Magdaline Bourbon
Source: Author's private collection

My mother, Magdaline Bourbon, was born in Dulhan Sahiba Palace at Lakherapura, Bhopal on 11 April 1903. She was the only daughter of Gasper Bourbon, alias Babbar Masih, and Rosina Bourbon (see the Bourbon family tree for more details). My mother's childhood was spent in Dulhan Sahiba Mahal, and she spent a good length of time with Nawab Sultan Jahan and the Begum's daughter-in-law, Maimoona Sultan. Magdaline Bourbon was a devout Catholic, like the other members of the Bourbon family. Schooled in an English-medium convent school in Sagar, Madhya Pradesh, she was fluent in English and Urdu, and was very fond of reading. She used to wear typical Bhopali clothes: *churidar pyjamas* and *Turki kurta* with a long *dupatta* of contrasting colours. She was fond of flowers, especially *bela* or *mogra*, which are small white flowers with a heavenly fragrance (Arabian jasmine or *Jasminum sambac*). Her *zarda* (tobacco) and *paan* (betel leaf) came specially from Lucknow. Before marriage, she observed strict *purdah* and covered herself with a long drape. Since childhood, my mother had heard stories about her family's history, starting from Jean Philippe de Bourbon's arrival in India. She often used to tell us this family history, and was very proud of her lineage.

In 1950, I visited the palace of Dulhan Sahib at Lakherapura with my mother. It was in the heart of the city and, at that time, Aijaz Masih resided there. It was in a very dilapidated state. Due to poor upkeep, it reflected little of its past glory. The palace was a huge structure with a tall wooden gate. It was built by Balthazar Bourbon, circa 1825, on the eastern side of Yasin Mahal. On the southern side of Yasin Mahal were the Imambara and Muhi Uddin mosque. It is also close to the mufti's house and the palace of Nawab Baqi Muhammad Khan, now called the Jahangiria School. Dulhan Sahib's palace situates her as a wealthy woman who possessed important fiefs and held high rank among the residents of Bhopal. In earlier days, Dulhan Sahib (Isabella Bourbon, wife of Balthazar Bourbon or Shahzad Masih) lived in this special palace built for the Bourbons. The first formal written description of the palace was by traveller and photographer Louis Rousselet, in *Le Fils du Connetable* (1882). When he visited Isabella de Bourbon, known in the court as Bourbon Sirdar, he was struck by her 'European style' of living and mentioned that 'I cannot describe my astonishment and surprise on hearing this account, which the [Bourbon] princess gave me.' (Rousselet 1875, 430). The resident priest who introduced Louis Rousselet to Dulhan Sahib said, 'I reside here in the capacity of chaplain of Madame Isabella de Bourbon, a Christian princess who holds

Dulhan Sahiba Mahal, Darwaza (gate) through which an elephant could pass
Source: Author's private collection

the first place of the kingdom after the Begum.' (Rousselet 1875, 428) At that time, Dulhan Sahib (1808–1882) would have been 66 years of age.

The next morning, Rousselet mounted an elephant and, accompanied by the priest, arrived at the Dulhan Sahiba Mahal. According to his description, though modest in appearance, the palace was quite sizeable. Rousselet was received by armed personnel who escorted him to a large salon on the first floor, where Bourbon Sirdar was waiting for him. Rousselet wrote that after a good handshake, 'I was struck by her type, which is eminently European, and by the clear yellow tint of her skin.'(Rousselet 1875, 429) Dulhan Sahib narrated her family history to Rousselet. She said they were the descendants of Jean de Bourbon. A clan of 400 families settled in Bhopal state. These people lived under Dulhan Sahib's leadership. Most families called themselves 'Frances,' a corruption of the word 'Frenchmen'.

Magdaline Bourbon was frequently invited to events that the Begums organized. Nawab Sultan Jahan Begum, ruler of Bhopal, and her daughter-in-law, Maimoona Sultan, wife of Nawab Hamidullah Khan, took special interest in Magdaline. Babbar Masih and his wife Rosina died very early, when their daughter Magdaline was very young, so the royal family looked after Magdaline's needs. The friendship between Nawab Sultan Jahan Begum and Magdaline lasted her entire lifetime. Sultan Jahan Begum and

Maimoona Sultan were keen to get my mother married to a suitable young man.

Born in Choubis Pargana region of West Bengal in 1875, my grandfather, Mr Bipin Bihari Ghosal, belonged to a Bengali Brahmin family. He later decided to follow the Christian faith, as he was very disenchanted by the Hindu caste system. He narrated his life story in an unpublished memoir called *My Homecoming*. A copy of this book is kept at the Loreto House Kolkata College Library. Bipin Ghosal was an

Mr Bipin Ghosal and Sir John Marshal at Sanchi
Source: Author's private collection

archaeologist by training under Sir John Marshal, Director General of the Archaeological Survey of India.

Bipin Ghosal was instrumental in drawing the attention of Sir John Marshall towards the magnificent Sanchi Stupas, which were his passion. In 1912, Sir John Marshall took up the restoration of the monuments there. Sanchi got a railway station through Mr Ghosal's persistent requests to the British. In acknowledgement of his commitment, hard work, knowledge, and documentation skills, Bipin Ghosal was later put in charge of the Sanchi Museum. More on this phase of his life can be found in the book *Sanchi Rediscovered*, by Susheila Ghosal. British rulers, royal dignitaries from other countries, and intellectual personalities of Bipin Ghosal's time had high appreciation for his work on Sanchi.

My grandfather's father, Babu Amarnath Ghosal, was secretary to the municipality of Mirzapur in the United Provinces, and enjoyed a position of good repute in society. My grandfather, Bipin Ghosal, received his master's degree in English Literature from Allahabad University and was a gold medalist. Bipin Ghosal began his career as a professor of English in Bhopal. After his education in Calcutta, he was appointed tutor to the Begums in Bhopal and taught them English language. He was then sent to Sanchi to read

Cover of Mr Bipin Ghosal's book
Source: Author's private collection

and preserve the documents of the monument. Later, he took charge of the King Edward Museum, Bhopal State. Below is a picture of Nawab Sultan Jahan Begum with HRH Edward, Prince of Wales, at the inaugural ceremony of King Edward Museum. Called Central Library today, it was no ordinary museum. Bipin Ghosal wanted it to reflect the lifestyles of the people of Bhopal. The museum was conceptualized to display the full range of artifacts that reflect the people of Bhopal. This included calling the weavers of Bhopal to showcase the process of making fine muslin cloth. Bhopal's famous *zari-zardosi*, embroidery done with gold and silver thread, was shown in the museum as well. The museum boasted a well-stocked library in those days. It was truly an *Ajaayab ghar*, which means a place with unique items.

After Magdaline married Satish Chandra Ghosal, son of Bipin Bihari Ghosal, she had to leave Bhopal

Nawab Sultan Jahan Begum with HRH Edward, Prince of Wales, at the inaugural ceremony of King Edward Museum. Source: https://cdn.images.express.co.uk/img/dynamic/galleries/x701/124655.jpg

Magdaline Bourbon
Source: Author's private collection

when her new husband got a job with the Scindias, the royal family of Gwalior. He became General Manager of the state transport company called the Gwalior & North India Transport (GNIT). GNIT was a bus service run by Maharaj Jivajirao Scindia. Magdaline did not want to leave Bhopal, so she went to Nawab Hamidullah Khan to seek advice. Nawab Sahib encouraged her to travel with her husband to Gwalior. He wanted Bhopali girls to go out of the state to broaden their horizons. But in those days, most Bhopal girls got married within the state and continued to live there. My mother was quite unhappy leaving Bhopal, and also worried about her monthly payment from the royal family. She used to receive a sum of Rs 30 per month for her upkeep. Nawab Hamidullah Khan promised that she would continue to receive this *mansab* wherever she was, and asked her to accompany her husband to Gwalior. Thereafter, every year before Christmas, Magdaline used to travel to Bhopal to get her due from the government treasury. Even after India's independence in 1947, this *mansab* continued. Magdaline was very proud that she belonged to the Bourbon family and used to love Bhopal; she also had a peaceful and happy marriage with Satish Ghosal.

During her lifetime, Magdaline Bourbon tried her best to maintain contact with the other branches of her paternal family. She used to meet her cousins,

Frank Bourbon (alias Hidayat Masih, married to Bertha) and Edwin Bourbon (alias Imtiaz Masih, married to Mazie). These Bourbons later migrated to Australia and I am still in touch with them. The girls of this branch of our family tree went to school and were very close with the girls of the royal family. Shaharyar Khan writes in *Begums of Bhopal*, 'Princess Abida Sultan, Sultan Jahan's granddaughter...recalls, her Bourbon school friends whose fair complexions and blue eyes set them apart from other schoolgirls. She recalls that their Christianity was never a negative factor' (Khan 2000, 65).

In Gwalior, Magdaline Bourbon met the Filose family, another French contingent who had travelled to and remained in India. The Filose family had a house near the Catholic Church of Gwalior. Mr Filose was an officer of high rank in the Gwalior Army. During the Dussehra festival procession, he used to sit on an elephant right behind the Maharaj Jivajirao Scindia's elephant. This was a great honour. Mr and Mrs Filose were Godparents to Magdaline's daughters. Magdaline and her husband were also very close to the royal family of Gwalior. They were invited to the events the Scindias used to organize. Once, Maharaj Jivajirao and Rani Vijaya Raje Scindia called all the *darbari* (coterie) for lunch. My parents were also invited. After lunch, my mother went into a corner and opened her *dibia* (a small box). While she was taking out her *paan* (betel leaf with nuts) to eat, the Maharaja and Maharani saw her and asked, 'Won't you give us some?' My mother immediately offered them a *paan* each. In the following days, ladies of the palace started carrying *paan* to please the royal family.

After having three daughters, Rani Sahiba Vijaya Raje Scindia was expecting a baby again. Rani Sahiba was from Nepal and Maharaj Scindia was from Maharashtra. All the ladies of the court had initially wanted the Maharaja to marry a girl from their community. It was said that if the Maharani gave birth to a girl again, for the sake of the throne, the Maharaja would have to marry someone else. Rani Sahib had only two close friends: Miss Filose, sister of General Filose, a Frenchwoman, and my mother, Magdaline Ghosal (née Bourbon). Rani Sahiba was under a lot of stress and asked Ms Filose and Madgaline to pray that she may have a baby boy. They used to console her by telling her not to worry and that she would have a baby boy this time. By the grace of God, a boy was born; they named him Madhavrao Scindia. Gwalior celebrated the birth of their next ruler for one whole week. A special *darbar* was called. By this time, my father had been given the title of Colonel and had to wear a Maharashtrian red *pagri* (turban), *angarkha* (a shirt with pleats), and *churidar pyjama*s (pants gathered tightly at the ankles) with a sword tied to the waist. He looked very handsome in his uniform. Madhavrao Scindia went on to become the Minister for Railways, then Tourism, Civil Aviation and finally Human Resource Development in several central governments between 1986 and 1996. Unfortunately Madhavrao Scindia met with an untimely death due to a plane crash in September 2001. It was a tragedy for the Scindias and unbearable news for my family.

I still remember the times when we four daughters and our household help used to sit by the fireplace in our house to listen to my mother's stories. My mother had beautiful memories of her childhood in Bhopal. The stories described valiant accounts of the Bourbon men and the very brave ladies of Bhopal. In those days, there was no television, so we would pass cold winter evenings listening to these stories and munching dry fruits and nuts. It was just after India's partition from Pakistan, and we had witnessed a lot of bloodshed. In the context of this uneasy calm, my mother tried to make things normal by reading some beautiful stories about her past to us. We all huddled together, eager to hear the stories. Often, she would read from a book of fantasy stories titled *Tilism-e-Hoshruba*, which had a vivid blue cover. It was the *Harry Potter* of our times.

Agra had seen a lot of riots around 1948, when my father was posted there. Refugees from Pakistan were settling down on the Indian side of the border, and Muslims from Agra were moving to Pakistan. We lost many friends in the process. The British were on their way out and wanted to visit Mughal monuments one last time. My father was a state official and considered it his duty to welcome all visitors and take them sightseeing. As children, we knew the history of these monuments very well due to our multiple visits. The most famous sites included Taj Mahal, Akbar's tomb at Sikandra, where Akbar and his wife Miriam Zamani were buried; Fatehpur Sikri, where Akbar used to live with his Begums and met all visitors, including the Jesuit Fathers who used to come from Goa and other places. During the time of Akbar, the Jesuit Fathers used to stay in the Ebadat Khaana (house of prayer), outside the walls of Fatehpur Sikri. This place was excavated by the Archeological Survey of India's officer Mohammed K. K. We were very young and were fascinated by the history that surrounded us in Agra.

As it is customary for Christians to go to the cemetery to pray for the dear departed, my mother used to take us to the Armenian cemetery in Agra to pray for the Bourbons buried there. We would take candles and accompany my mother on 2 November, All Souls Day. The old cemetery, known as Martyrs Graveyard, is in front of the Civil Court where the soldiers and Englishmen were buried. An Armenian community was massacred in one small room where they were praying, by the order of the Mughal King Aurangzeb. The victims are buried there in one of the oldest graveyards in India. The Bourbon graves were

Tombs of the Bourbons at the graveyard in Agra
Source: Author's private collection

platforms built with red stone, with typical Mughal-style architecture. The tombs still have Bourbon names inscribed on them.

Magdaline Bourbon often spoke about how the first Bourbon came to India, and she knew where her ancestors were buried. She had heard these stories from her family, and they match the narratives of other historians, several of whom I have quoted in this book. My mother resembled the other Bourbons in her family, with her fair complexion, light eyes, and incredible dignity. She was a rare fusion of the cultures of East and West. Her table manners were excellent and her living style was truly aristocratic. Her meals were served at the exact same time each day: breakfast at 8:30 am, lunch at 12:30 noon, and dinner at precisely 8:30 pm. The dinner table was always well laid, with a damask tablecloth, napkins, forks, spoons, and knives. She was a Roman Catholic Christian who was thoroughly enmeshed in Bhopali culture. While greeting others, she used the typical Muslim style of raising her hand to say '*Salaam*'.

The royal house of Bhopal gave the Bourbons special names to show their affection. My mother was given the name Middo Aapa. The graciousness of the royal family towards Magdaline continued even after her marriage when she left Bhopal. From her father, Babbar Masih, Magdaline inherited about 50 acres of land behind the *haveli* in the Motia Talao region. When she went to Gwalior with her husband, she decided to lease the land to Shamla Kothi Nawab Rashead Mia. In lieu of the leased land, Rashead Mia sent Magdaline Rs 500 per year. When her husband died in 1963, Magdaline came back to the Jagirdar Sahib in Bhopal and requested that he give back her land. He smiled and asked her 'What if I don't give back your land?' Mother folded her hands and said, 'Then I will go away'. Without saying a word, he got up and went into his inner chambers and brought out the land-related documents to give back to Magdaline. This land was about 50 acres located in the middle of Bhopal, now called Jehangirabad area. As time passed by, my mother donated part of this land to Mother Teresa, who needed a place to build the first Missionaries of Charity home in Bhopal. My relationship with the Missionaries of Charity thus began and grew stronger over the years.

When I began working on my master's thesis at St. John's College, Agra, on the topic of the advent of Christians in India, my mother asked me to research the history of the Bourbons of India. She handed me the photographs of my ancestors and made me promise that I will do my best to research and write about the forgotten Bourbons. Madgaline Bourbon, is no longer with us, but I have kept this promise—and I am deeply grateful for the experience.

THE FAMILY TREE OF THE BOURBONS IN INDIA AND THE LATER BOURBONS

In this chapter we trace the family tree of the Bourbons of Bhopal from the original ancestor down to the present day. The chapter can be read in association with the family tree, which appears as a chart at the end of the book.

Genealogy of the Indian Bourbons

Jean Philippe de Bourbon,* Count Clermont and Raja of Shergarh (1523-1592) claimed to be the natural born son of Charles III (1490-1527), who was also known as Connétable de Bourbon and Commander of the Holy Roman Emperor Charles V. The Connétable was married to Suzanne de Bourbon, a granddaughter of the King of France, Louis XI on 10 May 1505.

Jean Philippe de Bourbon
Source: Author's private collection

John Philippe de Bourbon arrived in India ca 1547, and was appointed an official at the court of the

*Names marked in bold indicate the direct ancestors of the author.

Mughal Emperor Akbar. At the Emperor's suggestion he was married to Juliana, the sister of Akbar's Christian queen Mariam Zamani in 1549. He served at the Mughal court with distinction for many years and died at Agra ca 1607, leaving behind two sons: 1. Alexander de Bourbon or Secunder Bourbon and 2. Saville Bourbon. All the Bourbons in India are descended from Jean Philippe de Bourbon.

1. Alexander de Bourbon or Secunder Bourbon was born in 1550. He was a friend and adviser to Emperor Jahangir. Alexander was later in-charge of Akbar's seraglio and companion to Jahangir. Not much is known about his marriage and his descendants.

2. **Saville Bourbon** was born in either 1560 or 1582 and married Miss Allemaine in either 1582 or 1600 and ruled from 1592 or 1607 till 1620.[1] His son was Alexander II de Bourbon or Secunder Bourbon, Raja of Shergarh. No more information is available regarding his other sons and descendants.

Alexander II de Bourbon or Secunder Bourbon, Raja of Shergarh, son of Saville Bourbon and Miss Allemaine, was born in 1605. He married Miss Robertson in 1640. His son was Anthony Bourbon.

Anthony Bourbon or Antoine of Bourbon, Raja of Shergarh (1646–1700 [approximate dates]) was the son of Alexander II and Miss Robertson. He married Miss Mericam or the granddaughter of Yaqub Khan an Afghan, and sister of Nawab Taqarrub Khan. He was the last man to hold charge of the Mughal Royal

Seraglio when Delhi was sacked by Nadir Shah in 1737. He also held the title of Nawab. He narrowly escaped from Delhi and took refuge in Shergarh. He had two sons and three daughters. His daughters were: A. Mary, B. Isabel and C. Catherine, and the sons were D. Francis Bourbon I or Fradi Bourbon, and E. Anthony Bourbon II.

A. Mary married Manuel Bervett.
B. Isabel—nothing further is known about her.
C. Catherine, married Aloysius (a Portuguese gentleman)
D. Anthony Bourbon II married a Portuguese lady. He had 6 children. His daughters were: 1. Mary, 2. Kathy, 3, Tuna (Maria), 4. Dominica, and the sons were: 5. Anthony III and 6. Francis.
  1. Mary, married Isa Khan
  2. Kathy, married Masita
  3. Tuna (Maria) alias Salabat-un-Nisa married Nawab Isa Khan (David). They had a son.
    i. James David
  4. Dominica married Nawab Yaqub Khan (Patrick) and died at Narwar. She had seven children, including two daughters and four sons.
    i. Hurmat-un-Nisa
    ii. Mary, married Loakine
    iii. Paul
    iv. Pedro
    v. Maud
    vi. Merrick Mian Masih Raza Khan, married Dominica
    vii. John, (wife's name not known), married and had a son.
      a. Manuel, married Catherine. They had a son.
        - Gasper
  5. Anthony III married Louisa. They had two daughters.
    i. Bourbon, married Jacob
    ii. G. Bourbon, married M. Burvett

6. Francis married Louisa Bervett, daughter of Dhamkane Bervett. They had two children.
    - i. Mary, married Pedro Bourbon
    - ii. Ignatus married Pascala De Silva, daughter of Pedro De Silva. They had four children—Catherine, Louisa, Marianne and Anthony.
        - a. Catherine, married Saville Bourbon alias Sarfaraz Masih
        - b. Louisa, married Anthony Bourbon alias Khairat Masih
        - c. Marianne married Balnit Francis. They had a daughter Arliel Begum
            - ◆ Arliel Begum married Bernet alias Falak Sahab. They had four daughters.
                - ☆ Daughter, died young
                - ☆ Caroline
                - ☆ Karbasiti Bernet
                - ☆ Marianne, married John Baptiste Filose
        - d. Anthony married Anthonia, daughter of John William. He had five children from Maria, to whom he was not officially married.
            - ◆ Anadi Bourbon, died after marriage
            - ◆ Samuel, married daughter of William Helm. They had a son.
                - ☆ Alexander (Secunder), died young
            - ◆ Juliana married Thomas Taut
            - ◆ Mary, wife of Captain Krishan Kaul. They had a daughter.
                - ☆ Louisa
            - ◆ Balthazar Bourbon married Marianne, alias Nargis, daughter of John. They had four children.
                - ☆ Jean Bourbon, married Bisnieth Jocain
                - ☆ Catherine, married John Molmes
                - ☆ John Bourbon
                - ☆ Anatalia, married Banet

The author and her family are descended from Francis Bourbon I. The line of descent of this part of the family is shown hereafter.

E. Francis Bourbon I, Raja of Shergarh, (lived 1680–1738; ruled 1689-1737). He married Louisa, alias Zaib-un-Nisa, an Armenian lady, in 1710. Francis Bourbon was said to be the Prince sovereign of Shergarh. Until the destruction of Delhi by Nadir Shah, Jean Philippe and four generations of his family had been with the Mughals. Francis Bourbon was the last man to hold charge of the Mughal Imperial Seraglio until the attack of Nadir Shah in 1739. He fled with all the members of the family and other Christians (about 300) to Shergarh. He had four children. (1) Fakhr-un-Nisa (2) Saville Bourbon (3) Francis Bourbon II, alias Sosher Bourbon and (4) Salvador Bourbon alias Ghulam Masih.

1. Fakhr-un-Nisa, married Saville Bcrvet
2. Saville Bourbon alias Fazal Masih (Panno) married Ana Khanum Armenian. They had four children.
   - i. Josine
   - ii. Anasia
   - iii. John Batis Bourbon, married Asad-un-Nisa
   - iv. Anthony. His wife's name is not known. They had a son.
     - a. Saville II. His wife's name is not known. They had three sons.
       - ◆ John Bourbon, married Miss Short, sister of Christian wife of King of Oudh
       - ◆ Simon Bourbon married (wife's name unknown) and had a son.
         - ☆ Osborne B.
       - ◆ Balthazar Bourbon. His wife's name is not known. They had four children.
         - ☆ Nathalie Bourbon, married Montere
         - ☆ John
         - ☆ Luis
         - ☆ Peter
3. Francis Bourbon II, alias Sosher Bourbon, alias Abdul Masih, alias Pak ji, was born in 1711 and married Nathalie Armenian in 1732. He was the Raja of Shergarh from 1738 to 1778. In 1778 the Raja of Narwar attacked the fort in order to obtain its possession. Many were massacred including Francis Bourbon II. He left behind two sons (i) Dominick Bourbon and (ii) Ignatus Bourbon.

i. Dominick Bourbon, alias Babbar Masih, married Marie, the daughter of Isa Khan and Salabat-un-Nisa. They had six children—two daughters and four sons.

a. Margaret, alias Najabat-un-Nisa, married Thomas

b. Maria Bibi, alias Umda Bibi, married Mirza Cain

c. Manuel Bourbon, alias Shuja'at Bahadur

d. Parlo Bourbon, alias Sher Afghan Masih

e. Pedro Bourbon, alias Huraiz Masih

f. John Bourbon married Jane, the daughter of Isa Khan. They had two sons.

- Tufail Bourbon
- Manuel Bourbon, alias Sarfaraz Masih, married Catherine, the daughter of Ignatus Bourbon, alias Anas. They had a son.
  - ☆ Gasper Bourbon

ii. Ignatus Bourbon, born 1734, married Pascala De Silva. They had one son.

a. Pedro Bourbon, alias Imdad Masih, was born in 1753. He was married to Miss A. Merrick, alias Hurmat-un-Nisa, alias Simi Bibi Anna, daughter of Salvador Merrick. She died in 1855 aged 100 years and was buried in Agra in the Armenian cemetery (Grave no. 162). Pedro Bourbon along with Salvador Bourbon, defended Bhopal during the Maratha siege, in 1812-13. He died in Bhopal in 1833 and was buried in Agra (Grave no. 163). Pedro and Harmat-un-nisa had five children—four daughters and a son.

- G. Bourbon, alias Izzat-un-Nisa, married Isa Raza Khan
- Zamarrud-un-Nisa, married J. Burvett
- Gumas-un-Nisa, alias Miss Masla, married Jacob
- Miss Anatalia, married Masih Ata Khan
- Anthony Bourbon, alias Khairat Masih, was born in 1785 and died in 1853. He was married to (1) Louisa Bourbon, alias Sunai (Simi) Bibi, daughter of De Silva and had children by (2) Gulab Masih (mistress) and (3) Ghasiti (mistress). He

had 10 children, five—Fazal Masih, Ghulam Masih, Bakshih Masih, Nawazish Masih and Pedro—from Sunai Bibi; one—Thomas Tress—from Gulab Masih; and four—Faiz Masih, Hidayat Masih, Francis and Yana—from Ghasiti.

The details of his children from Sunai Bibi are:

- ☆ Fazal Masih
- ☆ Ghulam Masih
- ☆ Bakshish Masih
- ☆ Nawazish Masih
- ☆ Pedro Bourbon alias Imdad Masih married (A) Annie Bourbon and (B) Catherine School. He had three children—(i) Louisa, (ii) Francisca, and (iii) Anthony—from Annie, and two children, (iv) John James and (v) Juliana from Catherine School.
    - (i) Louisa married Bervett and had five children
        - (a) John
        - (b) George
        - (c) Mary
        - (d) Merry
        - (e) William, married (wife's name unknown).
            - → 6 children
    - (ii) Francisca married Thomas Francis and had 3 children
        - (a) Eliza, married Anthony
        - (b) Dominica married Dr Sue, and had a son
            - → Francis De Sue
        - (c) Louis married (1) Claussy (2) Miss Anthony
            - → Winifred, from Claussy
            - → Son, from Miss Anthony
    - (iii) Anthony Bourbon was born in 1816. He was Captain of the Begum's house. He married (1) Frances Bernard (2) Ms Vincent and had five children—Rosa Mary from Frances; and Agnes, Catherine, Good Day and Eugene (who was blind) from Ms Vincent.

No more is known about his children from Miss Vincent. The details of his children from Frances Bernard are:

(a) Rosa Mary married Augustus Manuel, a Pleader of Lucknow and had eight children.

→ Annie married Claudius Bailey

→ Mary Agnes

→ Ellen William

→ Harriett, married Bailey

→ Caroline, was married and had a daughter Sangster, who married Jones, a Police Inspector in Bareilly

→ Edwin

→ Joseph

→ Charlotte had a son William, who had a son

(iv) John James, married Marcilena Magdalene Short and had 5 children.

(a) Kitty

(b) Peter Philip

(c) Victor Vincent

(d) Grace, married John Moses

(e) Jane, had five children

→ Joseph

→ Francis

→ Peter

→ Georgina

→ Agnes

(v) Juliana married Burvett, and had three children.

(a) William

(b) John alias Jacob, who had two children.

→ Margaret

→ Angelina

(c) Madeline married Louis Francis, and they had

five children. Their names were:

→ Harry

→ Albert

→ Alice

→ William

→ Agnes

Continuing with the direct descendants of the earlier Anthony Bourbon / Khairat Masih (1785–1853):

☆ Thomas Tress B. from Gulab Masih

☆ Faiz Masih from Ghasiti

☆ Hidayat Masih from Ghasiti

☆ Francis Bourbon from Ghasiti

☆ Yana from Ghasiti, married Salvador Smith and had three children.

(i) John Smith, married Maria Dolly

(ii) Mirza, married Miss Filose

(iii) William Smith, married Mariam and had two children

(a) Dominick Smith

(b) Daughter

We have just described the descendants of the family line of Francis Bourbon II. Now we trace the descendants of the last son of Francis Bourbon I, i.e. Salvador Bourbon.

4. **Salvador Bourbon,** alias Ghulam Masih, Raja of Shergarh, was born in 1736, the son of Francis Bourbon I and Louisa (Zaib-un-Nisa). He married Miss Burvett. Salvador was massacred in Narwar in 1779. He had three children—Sebastian, Dominica and Salvador.

i. Sebastian was killed at Narwar

ii. Dominica married Merrick, alias Mian Mirza Masih Raza Khan, son of Nawab Yaqub Khan

iii. **Salvador Bourbon**, alias Inayat Masih, was born in 1760. He fled from Narwar in 1779, took refuge in Gwalior and then came to Bhopal in 1785. He married Miss Thome in 1786. They had three children—Annie Begum, Philip, Pascala and an adopted son Balthazar. Salvador Bourbon died in Bhopal in December 1815.

a. Annie Begum, alias Billo Begum, alias Simi Begum Anna, is buried in Agra cemetery (Grave no. 162). She was married to Pedro, who was the son of John Bourbon, alias Mirza Yunus Beg. Annie Begum and Pedro had a son.
   - Johannes (Pedro II) Bourbon, alias Imdad Masih, married his first cousin Annie Francisca Bourbon, alias Banni Begum, alias Badshah Begum (daughter of Pascala Bourbon).* They had three daughters.
     - ☆ Magdaline
     - ☆ Daughter (name unknown)
     - ☆ Margherita Johannes, alias Umrao Begum / Sardar Begum, who married Manock John and had two sons.
       - (i) Pyare Sahab
       - (ii) Manock Moses, married Margherita Johannes, and had four sons.
         - (a) John
         - (b) Jacob
         - (c) Bonna Ventura
         - (d) Joseph Bernard Manuel, alias Dulare Sahab, who had a son.
           - → Bernard

b. Philip Bourbon, alias Imdad Masih, married Mary Smith and had five daughters.
   - Isabella Bourbon, married Mr Johannes
   - 4 daughters died young

c. Pascala Bourbon, alias Najib-un-Nisa, married Joseph Salvador Bourbon and had 6 children.
   - Alia
   - Julia

Right: Madame Dulhan

Extreme right: Balthazar Bourbon
Source: Author's private collection

- Fateh Bibi
- Shahzadi Khanum
- Anthony; he had two children
  - ☆ Aftab Begum
  - ☆ Hasid-un-Nisa
- Annie Francisca Bourbon, alias Banni Begum / Badshah Begum married her first cousin Johannes (Pedro II) Bourbon, alias Imdad Masih, and had three daughters. Their details have been given earlier (see * on p. 180 and in the chart).

a. **Balthazar Bourbon** alias Hakim Shahzad Masih was born in 1787 (1772). He died on 1 January 1829 in Bhopal and was buried in his own garden near Bhopal Talkies beside his father Salvador. He married Miss Isabella (Elizabeth) Johnstone alias Madame Dulhan (born in 1808). They were married probably in the year 1821, as she was only 21 when Shahzad Masih died, i.e. in 1829. Madame Dulhan died in Bhopal on 3 June 1882 and is buried in St. Francis Assisi Church at Jehagirabad, Bhopal. They had a daughter, Joana, and Madame Dulhan later recognized and also adopted his son Sebastian Bourbon.

- Joana Budhan, alias Bibi Huria, married Anthony De Silva, son of Hakim Don Alexius De Silva and Rosy Bennett. They

Right: Sebastian Bourbon and Joanna Bernard

Extreme right: Bonaventura Bourbon
Source: Author's private collection

had two children.

☆ Son (name unknown)

☆ Daughter (name unknown)

- **Sebastian Bourbon** was an adopted son from a Brahmin lady and Balthazar Bourbon. He was born in 1830, i.e. after the death of Balthazar. Madame Dulhan adopted Sebastian after Balthazar's death in 1829. He married Miss Joana Bernard and had one son, Bonaventura Bourbon.

  ☆ **Bonaventura Bourbon,** alias Inayat Masih, was born in 1849. He married Miss Veronica Aranj on 16 June 1866. Veronica, born ca 1852, died on 16 June 1943. They had six children. He died on 20 July 1894 due to poisoning. He had been suffering from ill health (skin disease) for some time due to the effect of the slow poison.

  (i) Safaraz Masih, born ca 1876 and died young in 1882 or 1884.

  (ii) Shahzadi Bibi, alias Anna Mary, born ca 1874, married Francis.

  (iii) Salvador III Philip Napoleon Bourbon (1869–1912), alias Imdad Masih, died childless. He adopted Magdaline Bourbon, his niece, the daughter of Gasper Bourbon who died at an early age.

  (iv) Balthazar Bourbon (1867-1899), alias Shahzad Masih, married Blanche Bourbon and had three children.

  (a) Juliana died young

  (b) Franck Bourbon, alias Hidayat Masih (1897–

Edwin Bourbon, Maizie and children

Middle: Gasper Bourbon

Top right: Magdaline Bourbon and S.C. Ghosal
Source: Author's private collection

1936), married Bertha and had three children.

→ Philip

→ Vivian

→ Blanche

(c) Edwin Bourbon, alias Imtiaz Masih (Manmad), was born in 1898, just before the death of his father. He married Mazie and had eight children.

→ Peter, married Pam Windy and had two children.

✠ Tonia

✠ Diedre

→ Charmain, is a nun

→ Yvonne, married Maurice Dunne. They live in Itarsi in Madhya Pradesh and we remain in touch. They have three children.

✠ Mrs Michelle Chadwick (daughter)

✠ Patrick Dunne (son)

✠ Mrs Kerri Ann Lobo (daughter)

→ Elwin

→ Philomena

→ Joan

→ Ian

→ Joseph

(v) **Gasper Bourbon,** alias Babbar Masih, was born on 15 July 15 1872. He died in 1905. He married Rosina Bourbon (1885–1921). They had one daughter.

(a) **Magdaline Bourbon** was born on 11 April 1903. She was married to S.C. Ghosal on 28 May 1936. She died on 13 March 1962 in Agra. They had four daughters.

→ Bella, born 8 July 1936, married on 27 Dec 1961 to Captain Ivan David. They have two children.

✠ Shabnam, born 18 Oct 1962; married 14 Oct 1986 to Sandeep Malhotra They have two children.

✡ Neharika Malhotra, born 4 Jan 1990.

✡ Anandini Malhotra, born 4 June 1998.

✠ Captain Satish David, born 10 Nov 1963; married on 19 Dec 1988 to Anuradha David. They have two children.

✡ Captain Sharad David, born 22 Oct 1991.

✡ Captain Abhishek David, born 17 Sept 1993.

→ Susheila Ghosal, born 1942, never married, died 4 October 2016.

→ Sheila Deb, 27 August 1945, married to Squadron Leader S.K. Deb. They have one son.

✠ Janak Deb

→ **Indira Ghosal**, born 3 August 1939; married Dr B.K. Iyengar on 18 January 1976. They have two daughters.

✠ Radhika Iyengar, born 1 Feb 1977; married to Sumit Haldar. They have two children.

✡ Asmi Haldar (born 1 January 2012)

✡ Swara Haldar (born 17 November 2016)

✠ Pooja Iyengar, born on 19th June 1978; married on 21 December 2008 to Lt. Colonel V. Raghuram. They have a son.

✡ Arjun Rao (born 5 May 2014)

(vi) Bonaventura Bourbon II alias Aijaz Masih was born on 31 March 1895, i.e. posthumously to his father. He was born after a gap of about 19 years since the birth of Sarfaraz Masih Bourbon in 1876. Bonaventura married Philomina Alexander and had six children. Philomina Bourbon was born in 1903 and died on 10 February 1964. Bonaventura died on 4 March 1960.

(a) Blanche Bourbon married Mr Mascaranius. They had one daughter.

→ Francis Mascaranius Malhotra (currently resides in London)

(b) Adeline Bourbon

(c) Elline Bourbon, married Mr Gupta

(d) Sheila Bourbon married Mr Cherian

(e) John Bourbon, alias Iftikhar Masih

(f) Salvador Bourbon, alias Mumtaz Masih, born 1917 died 1978, married Matilda Green (1869-1894). They had five children.

→ Magdaline, married Constantine W. Lobo (currently resides in Bhopal)

→ Tressa, married Solomon (currently resides in Bhopal)

→ Veronica Bourbon married Peter Charan (currently resides in Bhopal). They have two children.

✠ Sonia Peter, married Victor

✠ Sharon Peter, married Johnson

→ Dr Iris Bourbon married Satyajit Daniel (currently resides in the US). They have two children.

✠ Joshua Daniel

✠ Shireen Daniel

→ Balthazar IV, born 1958, married Elisha Pachera, and has three children (currently resides in Bhopal)
   ✠ Frederick
   ✠ Adrian
   ✠ Michelle

Many members of this branch of the family still live in Bhopal. We have remained close to each other over the years. We often meet at marriages and church gatherings. The family tree includes all the Bourbon descendants. I do not vouch for any branch to be the 'true' Bourbons. Since I am re-creating a long-lost history, I am including all the branches that I know from my mother and from my extended family. The tree merely provides a bird's-eye view of all the relations of whom I am aware. I am still in touch with most of them.

The Later Bourbons

BONAVENTURA BOURBON

Bonaventura Bourbon, alias Inayat Masih, was born in 1849. He was the only son of Sebastian and Joanna Bernard Bourbon (Sardar Bahu). Most of his childhood was spent in Ichhawar with his father, Sebastian and his grandmother Dulhan Sahib. He was educated under the guidance of Dulhan Sahib and showed signs of a princely upbringing. He grew up as a *Jagirdar* (one who owns a feudal land grant) following the Bhopali Nawab's tradition. He portrayed himself as *Jagirdar* and a Nawab but also continued to showcase the blended Indo-French lifestyle.

Bonaventura Bourbon with his sons and daughter
Source: Author's private collection

Since childhood, Inayat Masih witnessed the loyalty of Dulhan Sahib and Sebastian Bourbon towards the royal family of Bhopal State and their sense of acumen in taking decisions. He had seen and met many Europeans and British officials visiting his grandmother Dulhan Sahib, especially during the Uprising of 1857 (when Sir Conrad and his troop were safely escorted by the Bourbons to Ichhawar). Inayat Masih grew up in Shaukat Mahal and later in Dulhan Sahiba ka Mahal and the Haveli in Jehangirabad. Inayat Masih married Miss Veronica Aranj in 1866. She was only 14 at that time. Dulhan Sahib gave her the name Sultan Bahu. Dulhan Sahib even educated her and got her acquainted with the Bourbon style of living. Bonaventura Bourbon and Sultan Bahu later on went to have six children.

Bonaventura Bourbon, with his children and attendants
Source: Author's private collection

Bonaventura's eldest son was Balthazar Bourbon born in 1867, alias Shahzad Masih, who married Blanche Bourbon. Shahzad Masih died very young at the age of 32 in 1899. He had three children: Juliana, Frank and Edwin. Bonaventura Bourbon's second son was Salvador III Philip Napoleon Bourbon, alias Imdad Masih. He was born three years after marriage i.e. in 1869. He died childless at the age of 43 on 11 July 1912. The third son was Gasper Bourbon alias Babbar Masih, who was born in 1872 and married Rosina Bourbon. He also died very young at the age of 33 in the year 1905, leaving behind his only child, Magdaline Bourbon, my mother. After three sons, Inayat Masih had a daughter born in 1874. Her birth was much celebrated and she was lovingly called by all as *shehzadi* or princess. Her name was Anna Mary alias Shehzadi Begum. My mother used to say that she was a very beautiful lady. She used to stay in Dulhan Sahiba Mahal along with her family. It is believed that a spirit used to come to meet her and he told her not to get married. So she decided not to get married. In those days people used to be superstitious. She used to always imagine that someone was in love with her. Whenever she needed something, the spirit used to come and help her and she never married. She used to look after her brother's son, her nephew, as her own son. My mother used to call Anna Mary 'Pupho' (a Muslim name for father's sister). After her, Inayat Masih had a boy named Sarfaraz Masih in 1876, but he died at an early age of 8 years.

In the picture on the facing page, probably taken around the year 1883, Bonaventura Bourbon alias Inayat Masih, poses with all his sons and daughter excluding his youngest son who was not born yet, Aijaz Masih. They have their attendants standing behind them. It is said that Bonaventura developed some kind of disease because of which his legs were paralyzed making him bedridden. His young sons took care of the father's business. Bonaventura died on 20 July 1894. There is a rumour that he was poisoned, which was the cause of the disease that affected his legs and stomach eventually causing his death. Bonaventura was very sick before his death. In the picture he is wearing socks as his feet were affected by the slow poison. After his death, his wife Veronica Aranj alias Sultan Bahu informed everyone of her pregnancy. According to Magdaline Bourbon, daughter of Gasper Bourbon, ladies of Dulhan Sahib's Mahal (palace) spoke about the unlikeliness of Veronica conceiving during Bonaventura's last

The children of Edwin Bourbon (Imtiaz Masih) Source: Author's private collection

days. A son was born posthumously on 31 March 1895 i.e. eight months and 10 days after the death of Bonaventura Bourbon. These dates are recorded as per the Catholic Church, Jehangirabad Bhopal. He was named Bonaventura, alias Aijaz Masih. It is said that Nawab Shahjahan Begum came to visit Veronica and after looking at the dark complexion of the baby she asked Sultan Bahu about the colour of the skin not resembling anyone from the Bourbon family. She didn't have an answer for Nawab Shahjahan Begum. There was further investigation, but no one could deny that the baby was not hers, therefore finally the baby was accepted. Aijaz Masih also received his part of the inherited *jagir* from the father's side.

According to Kincaid 'Intermarriage with individuals of Oriental race appears to have in no way detracted from their mental or physical capacity, though it has darkened their complexions' (1887). It appears that the typical Indian complexion started with Aijaz Masih, the last son of Bonaventura Bourbon. Bonaventura Bourbon had in all six children, Balthazar Bourbon, Salvador III, Gasper Bourbon, Sarfaraz Masih, Shehzadi Bibi alias Anna Mary, and Bonaventura Bourbon II, alias Aijaz Masih (born posthumously). The rest of the Bourbons had a typical European appearance and complexion. Balthazar's children were Juliana, Frank and Edwin. Edwin had eight children Peter, Charmain, Yvonne, Elwin, Philomena, Joan, Ian and Joseph. They were all fair and had blue eyes. Even the Princess of Bhopal Abida Sultan, studying in school, remarked about the Bourbon girls having blue eyes and fair complexions. This side of the family now resides in Australia. We still keep in touch through emails and phone. Recently the family visited London to commemorate Charmain's fifty years as nun. Members of the family including Joseph, Yvonne, Elwin, Joan, Philomena, Peter and Ian also joined the celebration (picture on the facing page).

GASPER BOURBON

Gasper Bourbon, alias Babbar Masih, was the third son of Bonaventura Bourbon, alias Inayat Masih. He was born on 15 July 1872. His mother was Veronica Rose Mary Bourbon. He was baptized on 23 July 1872, as per records at the St. Francis of Assisi Cathedral. His grandfather, Sebastian Bourbon, was his Godfather and his grandmother, Dulhan Sahib, was his Godmother. He was only six years of age when he lost

Gasper Bourbon with an attendant Source: Author's private collection

his grandfather, Sebastian Bourbon, in 1878. Soon after, when he was 10 years old, Dulhan Sahib passed away. Gasper alias Babbar Masih till then had received the guidance of Dulhan Sahib and Sebastian Bourbon. Like all other Bourbons, he was tall and handsome. He was well trained from early on to manage the administration of his *jagir*. He went on to marry Rosina Bourbon of the Alexander family in the year 1901. This was just after the coronation of Nawab Sultan Jahan Begum.

Their only daughter Magdaline Maria Bourbon was born on 11 April 1903. According to Magdaline Bourbon, Gasper Bourbon (Babbar Masih) was a very brave man. They used to live in the *haveli* (palace) of Jehangirabad, built by Balthazar Bourbon. Gasper Bourbon (Babbar Masih) inherited land after his father's death similar to other brothers, Salvador III (Imdad Masih) and Bonaventura (Aijaz Masih), amounting to rupees 3,000 each. The property of Gasper was around 52.10 *bigha*s (a unit of land measurement) amounting to rupees 3,327, which included property in Bilqisganj, Raisen, Ichhawar and Tehsil Huzur according to the agreement of 1299 Hijra i.e. 1882 AD, at the time of his death in 1905. While his other brothers passed away—Salvador III died childless in 1912, Sarfaraz Masih had a very short life (died in 1882 or 84) and Balthazar in 1899, Magdaline inherited the property of her father which was in the heart of the city.

But there was no account of the land in Bilqisganj, Raisen, Ichhawar and Huzur. The tradition at that time was that the property of the deceased was first taken back and included in the property of the state and then a fresh agreement needed to be signed by the city administrators for new allotment and distribution to the sons and daughters of the deceased.

Behind the Bourbon-owned Jehangirabad Haveli lived the Bhoies tribe of fishermen who used to catch the fish in Motia Talab or lake. According to Magdaline Bourbon, a fisherman once came crying to Gasper and asked him to save his child. When Babbar Masih reached the spot, he saw a child holding a big snake which was coiled round him. The child was dipping the snake's head in a bowl of milk, and asking him to drink it. Gasper instructed the father to stand behind the child, and told him as soon he (Gasper) caught the snake, the father should pick up the child. Gaspar caught the snake and pulled it, threw it outside the hut, and then killed it. Thus the child was saved. In a true sense he was the *Jagirdar*, and used to look after his people. His only daughter was Magdaline Bourbon, my mother, to whom I dedicate this book.

Endnote

1. The dates of Saville Bourbon's birth (1582) and marriage (1600) are as mentioned by Ram Babu Saksena (1941). According to the family's descendants, 1560 is the approximate date of his birth, correlating other events. Similarly with his marriage and death.

REFERENCES

Abu al-Fazal ibn Mubarak. 1873. *The Ain i Akbari*. Trans. by H. Blochmann. Calcutta: Asiatic Society of Bengal.

Bernacchioni, Raphael. 1918. *History of the Archdiocese of Agra*, J.N. Suares Codialbail Press, Mangalore [], as cited in Felix, O. C. The Rev. Father. 1918. 'Mughal Farmans, Pjis and Sanads issued in favour of the Jesuit Missionaries,' *Journal of the Punjab Historical Society*, Volume V. Calcutta: Printed at the Baptist Mission Press and Published by the Panjab Historical Society, Lahore.

Butler, John Francis. 1979. *Christianity in Asia and America after A.D. 1500*. Leiden: E.J. Brill.

Correia-Afanso, John. 1955. *Jesuit Letters and Indian History*. Indian Historical Research Institute, Bombay: St. Xavier's College.

Diver, Maud. 1942. *Royal India: A descriptive and historical study of India's fifteen Principal States and their rulers*. New York, London: D. Appleton Century Company.

Fanthome, Federic. 1895. *Reminiscences of Agra*. [Second Edition] Calcutta: Thacker, Spink and Co.

Felix, O. C. The Rev. Father. 1918. Mughal Farmans, Pjis and Sanads issued in favour of the Jesuit Missionaries, *Journal of the Punjab Historical Society*, Volume V. Calcutta: Printed at the Baptist Mission Press and Published by the Panjab Historical Society, Lahore.

Fisher, Michael and William Dalrymple, eds. 2007. *Visions of Mughal India: An Anthology of European Travel Writing*. London: I.B. Tauris & Company.

Haig, Lt Col. Sir, W. 1937. *The Cambridge History of India in Six Volumes – Vol. IV. The Mughal Period,* Cambridge: Cambridge University Press.

Hamid, Razia; Sultan, Rafat. 1986. *Bourbons: Nuqoosh-e-Bhopal.* Bhopal: Babul Uloom.

Hosten, H. The Rev. 1916. *Memoirs of the Asiatic Society of Bengal,* Part 11, Vol. V. No. 4.

Jahan, Sultan. 1929. *Tazkira-i-Baqi,* trans. Rashiduzzafar Khan, Calcutta: Thacker's Press and Directories, Ltd.

Khan, Shaharyar. 2000. *The Begums of Bhopal: A dynasty of women rulers in Raj India.* London: I.B. Tauris Publishers.

Kincaid, Charles Augustus. 1908. *The Tale of the Tulsi Plant and other Stories.* Bombay: The Times of India Office.

Kincaid, Colonel. 1887. 'The Indian Bourbons.' *The Asiatic Quarterly Review,* Edited by Demetrius Boulger, Volume III, January–April: 164–177.
https://archive.org/stream/in.ernet.dli.2015.530442/2015.530442.asiatic-quarterly_djvu.txt

Kochhar, R. K. 1994. Secondary tools of empire: Jesuit men of science in India. In T. R. de Souza (Ed.), *Discoveries, missionary expansion and Asian cultures.* New Delhi: Concept Publishing Company.

Lambert-Hurley, Siobhan. 2007. *Muslim Women, Reform and Princely Patronage: Nawab Sultan Jahan Begam of Bhopal.* London: Routledge.

Maclagan, Edward. 1932. The Indian Bourbon. In *The Jesuits and the Great Mogul,* pp. 162–166. London: Burns, Oates & Washbourne.

Malcolm, Sir John. 1824. *A Memoir of Central India, including Malwa and Adjoining Provinces,* London: Kingsbury, Parbury & Allen.
https://archive.org/stream/amemoircentrali05malcgoog/amemoircentrali05malcgoog_djvu.txt

Malleson, G. B. 1984. *History of the French in India: from the founding of Pondicherry in 1674 to the capture of that place in 1761.* London: W.H. Allen & Co.

Preckel, Claudia. 1980. The Roots of Anglo-Muslim Cooperation and Islamic Reformism in Bhopal. *History Today.* 30 (October): 31, 92.

Prince Michael of Greece. 2008. *Le Rajah Bourbon.* Vanves Cedex: Le Livre de Poche.

Raj, Fr. Felix. n.d. *Jesuits at Akbar's Court,* Kolkata: The Goethal Indian Library and Research Society.

Robinson, Francis. n.d. 'The Begums of Bhopal', Introduction by Princess Abida Sultan of Bhopal, http://apps.engr.utexas.edu/ethics/standards/bhopal/The%20 Begums%20of%20Bhopal.pdf

Rousselet, Louis. 1882. *Le Fils du connétable*. Paris: Hachette.

Rousselet, Louis and Charles Randolph Buckle. 1875 [reprint 1975]. *India and its Native Princes: travels in Central India and in the presidencies of Bombay and Bengal.* London: Bickers & Son.

Saksena, Ram Babu. 1941. *European and Indo-European Poets of Urdu and Persian*. Lucknow: Newul Kishore Press.

Seth, Mesrovb Jacob. 1897. *History of the Armenians in India, from the Earliest Times to the Present Day*, London: Luzac and Co., Publishers to the India Office, 46 Great Russell Street. https://archive.org/stream/in.ernet.dli.2015.500613/2015.500613.Armenians-In_djvu.txt

Shahjahan, Begum of Bhopal, H.H. the Nawab. 1876. *Taj-ul-Ikbal Tarikh Bhopal, The History of Bhopal*. Trans. H.C. Barstow. Calcutta: Thacker, Spink and Co.

Sikandar Begum, Nawab of Bhopal. 1870. *A Pilgrimage to Mecca*. Trans. Elizabeth Willoughby-Osborne. London: Wm. H. Allen.

Sultan Jahan, Begum. 1918. *Hayat-i-Qudsi: Life of the Nawab Gauhar Begum alias the Nawab Begum Qudsia, of Bhopal*, Trans. W.S. Davis. London: Kegan Paul, Trench, Trubner & Co. Ltd. https://archive.org/stream/hayatiqudsilifeo00sulthayatiqudsilifeo00sult_djvu.txt

———. 1910. *An Account of my Life*, Vol. I. Trans. C.H. Payne. London: John Murray.

.1922. *An Account of my Life*, Vol. II. Trans. Abdus Samad Khan. Bombay: Times Press.

———.1922. *Al Hijab or Why Purdah is Necessary*. Calcutta: Thacker, Spink and Co.

Zaman, Taymiya R. 2012. Visions of Juliana: A Portuguese Woman at the Court of the Mughals. *Journal of World History*, Volume 23, Number 4, December: 761–91.

Other sources

Archaeological Survey of India (ASI), *Archaeological Survey of India Reports, Volume 2*, Office of the Superintendent of Government Printing, 1871. Original from the University of Michigan, Digitized 30 Jul 2009.

'Father Manoel da Fonseca, S.J M in Ava (1613–1652)'. Translated by the late Rev. L. Besse, S.J. Annotated and Edited by the Rev. H. Hosten. S.J. (1916) *Journal and Proceedings of the Asiatic Society of Bengal*, New Series, Vol XXI, 1925.

Bhopal State Gazetteer vol.3. 1908. Compiled by Captain C.E. Luard, Superintendent Gazetteer in Central India. Superintendent Government Printing, India. Assisted by Munshi Kudrat. https://archive.org/stream/in.ernet.dli.2015.123735/2015.123735.Bhopal-State-Gazetteer-Vol-Iii_djvu.txt

Imperial Gazetteer of India. 1908-1931. v. 13, p. 324. Oxford: Clarendon Press. Accessed at: Digital South Asia Library. http://dsal.uchicago.edu/reference/gazetteer/pager.html?objectid=DS405.1.I34_V13_330.gif

National Archives of India, Bhopal. Various reports, Retrieved from January 2015.

APPENDIX I: BHOPAL'S RULERS AND THE BOURBONS

Bhopal's Rulers	Contemporary Bourbons
MAMOLA BEGUM (ca 1715-1795) Was de facto ruler for about 50 years during the reigns of her stepsons, Faiz Mohammad Khan and Hayat Mohammad Khan.	Salvador Bourbon / Inayat Masih (1760–1815), came to Bhopal in 1785 and served as general in the Bhopal State Army. His cousin Pedro Bourbon (d. 1833) served as Commander of the Cavalry of Bhopal.
FAIZ MOHAMMAD KHAN (1731–1777) Ruled from 1742 to 1777.	
HAYAT MOHAMMAD KHAN (1735–1807) Ruled from 1777 to 1807.	
GHOUS MOHAMMAD KHAN (1767–1826) Ruled in 1807.	Balthazar Bourbon/Shahzad Masih, (1787 [1772?]–1829), was a Minister of Wazir Mohammad Khan, and adviser to Nazar Mohammad Khan and Qudsia Begum. His wife Madam Dulhan played an important role as a leader of the Christian community and lady in waiting to the Begums.
WAZIR MOHAMMAD KHAN (1766–1816) Ruled from 1807 to 1816.	
NAZAR MOHAMMAD KHAN (1791–1819) Ruled from 1816 to 1819.	

QUDSIA BEGUM
(1801–1881) Ruled from 1819 to 1837.

JAHANGIR MOHAMMAD KHAN
(1816–1844) Ruled from 1837 to 1844.

SIKANDAR BEGUM
(1816–1868) Ruled from 1844 to 1868.

Sebastian Bourbon / Meherban Masih
(1830–1878), became Prime Minister to Sikandar Begum in 1857.

SHAHJAHAN BEGUM
(1838–1901) Ruled from 1868 to 1901.

Bonaventura Bourbon I / Inayat Masih
(1849–1894).

SULTAN JAHAN BEGUM
(1858–1930) Ruled from 1901 to 1926.

Gasper Bourbon / Babbar Masih
(1872–1905).

NAWAB HAMIDULLAH KHAN
(1895–1960) Ruled from 1926 to 1960.

Magdaline Bourbon (1903–1962), received a pension from Bhopal's rulers.

APPENDIX II

Chapter 1

ARRIVAL OF JEAN PHILIPPE DE BOURBON IN AKBAR'S COURT

(TUGHRA) ROYAL MANDATE FROM JALAL-UD-DIN MUHAMMAD AKBAR

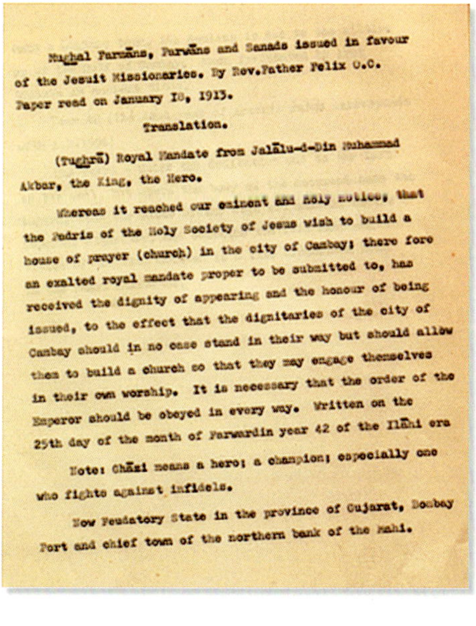

Mughal Farmāns, Parwāns and Sanads issued in favour of the Jesuit Missionaries. By Rev.Father Felix O.C. Paper read on January 10, 1913.

Translation.

(Tughrā) Royal Mandate from Jalālu-d-Din Muhammad Akbar, the King, the Hero.

Whereas it reached our eminent and holy notice, that the Padris of the Holy Society of Jesus wish to build a house of prayer (church) in the city of Cambay; there fore an exalted royal mandate proper to be submitted to, has received the dignity of appearing and the honour of being issued, to the effect that the dignitaries of the city of Cambay should in no case stand in their way but should allow them to build a church so that they may engage themselves in their own worship. It is necessary that the order of the Emperor should be obeyed in every way. Written on the 25th day of the month of Farwardin year 42 of the Ilāhi era

Note: Ghāzi means a hero; a champion; especially one who fights against infidels.

Now Feudatory State in the province of Gujarat, Bombay Port and chief town of the northern bank of the Mahi.

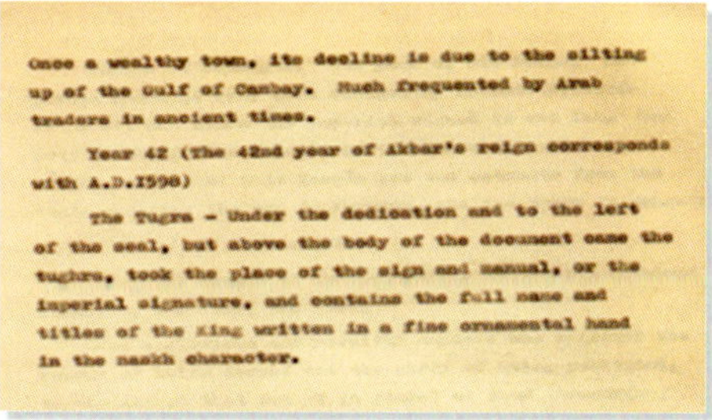

Once a wealthy town, its decline is due to the silting up of the Gulf of Cambay. Much frequented by Arab traders in ancient times.

Year 42 (The 42nd year of Akbar's reign corresponds with A.D.1598)

The Tugra - Under the dedication and to the left of the seal, but above the body of the document came the tughra, took the place of the sign and manual, or the imperial signature, and contains the full name and titles of the King written in a fine ornamental hand in the naskh character.

Mughal Farmans, Parwans and Sanads issued in favour of the Jesuit Missionaries, By Rev. Father Felix O.C. Paper read on January 10, 1913. (Original is kept in Archbishop Library, Agra. Translation of original Farman.)

(TUGHRA) ROYAL MANDATE FROM JALAL-UD- DIN MUHAMMAD AKBAR, THE KING, THE HERO

TRANSLATION

Whereas it reached our eminent and holy notice, that the padres of the Holy Society of Jesus wish to build a house of prayer (Church) in the city of Cambay: therefore an exalted royal mandate proper to the submitted to, has received the dignity or appearing and the honour of being issued, to the effect that the dignitaries of the city of Cambay should in no case stand in their way but should allow them to build a church so that they may engage themselves in their own worship. It is necessary that the order of the Emperor should be obeyed in every way. (Written on the 25th day of the month of Farwardin year 42 of the Ilahi era)

Note: Ghazi means a hero: a champion; especially one who fights against infidels.

[Cambay] Now feudatory State in the Province of Gujrat, Bombay Port and chief town of the northern bank of the mahi, once a wealthy town, and its decline is due to the silting up of the Gulf of Cambay. Much frequented by Arab traders in ancient times.

Year 42 (The 42nd year of Akbar's reign corresponds with A.D. I598)

The Tugra- Under the dedication and to the left of the seal, but above the body of the document came the tughra, took the place of the sign and manual, or the imperial signature, and contains the full name and titles of the king written in a fine ornamental hand in the naskh character.

Farman of Jahangir, 4th year of His Reign. The Farman which is very much damaged by insects measures 25″x8″, and bears the imperial tughra in red ink. The body of the Farman consist of ten lines in nastaliq. On the reverse of this Farman are two paragraphs extracted from the state records; the one in Persian, and the other in Marathi.

(TUGHRA) FARMAN OF ABU-I- MUSAFFAR NUR-UD-DIN MUHAMMAD JAHANGIR, THE KING, THE HERO

TRANSLATION

Now a glorious and merciful mandate has received the honour of being issued and the glory of being published, to the effect that out of (a piece) of land (measuring) six bighas, three bighas from the Mauza of Agra, for the autumn harvest of the year Takhaqugil (the year of the cook) in the way of inam (gratuity) to the Farangis (Europeans) for purposes of a garden and cemetery should be sanctioned and delivered over to them. The *Jagirdar*s and the Karoris (tax-gatherers) of the present and future is preservation and confirmation of this holy and exalted order.... having left (the land) in their possession (should never make) any change or alteration to it (and they should not burden them with expenses like) peshkash or jaribana, or zabitana or maharana, or daroghana or muhassilana, ... or qanungoi or (ordinance against niza) and takerar-i-zira at an all fiscal exactions- and they should make no demand and should regard them as freed and exempted in every way. They should not require) every year a fresh Farman and parwanchah... they (the authorities) should know it as their duty (written on) the 2nd of the month of Aban (in the 4th year (of the Emperor's reign) Note: This is the tenth year of the 12 year cycle known as the Aighur Era, see Jarrett's *Ain-i-Akbari*, Vol II PP. 20-21

Inam, or property, it denotes lands given for benevolent purposes. Such lands were hereditary. Peshkash, a magnificent present such as is only presented to princes, great men, superiors, etc. Jaribana is a rate imposed on the inhabitants of a district defraying the charges of measurement. See Steingass's *Persian English Dictionary*, P. 361. Zabitana, a fee exacted by the police officers. Mahrana, a fee exacted by the Qazi from the Muhammadans at weddings. (Steingass's P.E. Dicty. 1354)

(Fees of a darogha who was magistrate of a town or village) See Burhan (*Tatimmah* p. 40) Muhassilana- fees of the bailiff, or tax gatherer. Qanungoi – is the office of a ganungo in India, who is an officer whose duty it is to register and expand the laws of the empire. Aban (October) is the Persian name of the 8th lunar month corresponding with Hindu Kartik.

The Farman is kept in the archives of the Catholic mission in Agra.

PARWANAH FROM AURANGZEB OR ALAMGIR, WITH THE SEAL OF ASAD KHAN

TRANSLATION

Iah Asad Khan, the servant of king Alamgir, the Hero, 1103- The present and future officers of the Capitation tax (taken from) the zimis residing in the permanently established capital Akbarabad, should know that before this, according to the account book of the late Ruhullah Khan regarding the exemption of the capitation tax from five padris in number with their dependents, a parwanah to the address of late Shaikh Muhammand Sa'id, the late Amin of the capitation tax of that place, had been written. Nowadays the vakil (agent) of the Padris (has made) a request that the present Amin asks for a sanad (addressed) to his own name, He (the vakil) hopes that a parwanah to the address of the present and future officers of the capitation tax of that place will be given, It is therefore Ordered that in the matter of taking the capitation tax from Rator and other Padris, whose names are written in a marginal note, they according to the former order should not hinder them (the padris). In this matter they should take as much care as possible, Dates 9th of the month Jamada-us-Sani, 37th year of the exalted accession. On the Reverse is abstract of parwanah to the name of Father Rator and other priests: that according to the order of the king they are exempted from the expiation tax. Five padris in number with their dependents Padri Rator, Padri Michael, Padri John Emmanuel, Padri Anas, Padri Diuk. On the 11th day of Jamada-us-Sani in the 37th year it was entered in the Govt. account register.

It is according to the orders and according to the register. It has been seen.

Notes: Iah or lahu, 'He' or 'God'

(Asad Khan, father of Zulfiqar Khan, - In the 15th year of Aurangzeb's reign he was raised to the rank of 4000 and after a few years to the office of Vazir. Zimmi, one tolerated by the Muhammadan law, on paying an annual poll-tax; a Christian or a Jew. Ruhullah Khan was the Mir Bakhsh or Pay Master General. Kept in the Archives of the Catholic Missions at Agra.

The next two Farmans of Jahangir throw light on the fortune of the Christians at Ahmadabad; the one (No.III measuring 3'x15') gave permission for the building of a church there—while the other (No. Iv 27"x15") directed the local authorities to turn some Englishman out of the padre's lodging.

Chapter 3
THE BOURBONS OF BHOPAL

REFERENCE OF ICHHAWAR IN *THE IMPERIAL GAZETTEER OF INDIA*, V. 13, P. 324.

Ichchapuram Tahsil

Ichchapuram Town ('City of desire')- in the Berhampur *taluk* of Ganjam District, Madras, situated in 19° 7' N. and 84° 42' E., on the trunk road and on the East Coast Railway, 15 miles south-west of Berhampur. Population (1901), 9,975. It was formerly the headquarters of the Ichchapuram district of Chicacole*Sarkar*, and the seat of the Muhammadan Naib. Some small mosques in ruins alone remain. To one of these followers of the Prophet come from distant places for prayer. The place is now the head-quarters of a deputy-*tahsildar*.

Ichhawar—Town in the Nizamat-i-Maghrib or western district of Bhopal State, Central India, situated in 23° 2′ N. and 77° 1′ E. Population (1901), 4,352. The site is an old one, the present town having been built on the foundations of the village of Lakshmipura. A small fort in the place was built by the Marathas, who seized it in 1716. Ichhawar was made over to the Bhopal State under the Treaty of 1818. The Ichhawar*tahsil* was for many years held in *jagir* by the Bhopal Bourbons, who have given a succession of shrewd councillors and valiant soldiers to the State. About 1560 Jean Philippe Bourbon of Navarre, a cousin of Henry IV, came to India. He entered the service of Akbar, married Juliana, said to have been a sister of Akbar's `Christian wife,' and was created a Nawab. The family continued in the service of the Delhi emperors till 1739, when on the sack of that city by Nadir Shah they fled to the fort of Shergarh (25° 35′ N. and 77° 58′ E.), which they held in. *jagir* in the territory of the Narwar chief. The family remained in Narwar in safety till 1778, when the Raja, who was jealous of his powerful feudatory, attacked Shergarh and massacred all but four of the family, who managed to escape to Gwalior. After the capture of Gwalior in 1780 by Major Popham, some territory was assigned to them, and soon after Salvador Bourbon took service in the Bhopal State, and became a general in the State army. Salvador's son Balthasar was minister to Wazir Muhammad, and was instrumental in concluding the Treaty of 1818 with the British Government, he being one of the signatories. During the Mutiny of 1857 the fugitives from Agar *[sic]* were hospitably received by Jean de Silva and several of the Bourbon family who were then residing in the town. Members of the family still live in the State'.

Narwar chief. The family remained in Narwar in safety till 1778, when the Raja who was jealous of the powerful feudatory, attacked Shergarh and massacred all but four of the family who managed to escape to Gwalior. After the capture of Gwalior in 1780 by Major Popham. Some territory was assigned to them and soon after Salvador Bourbon took service in the Bhopal State and became a general in the State army. Salvador's son Balthazar was minister to Wazir Muhammad, and was instrumental in concluding the Treaty of 1818 with the British Government he being one of the signatories.

'*Asiatic Quarterly Review* 1887.'

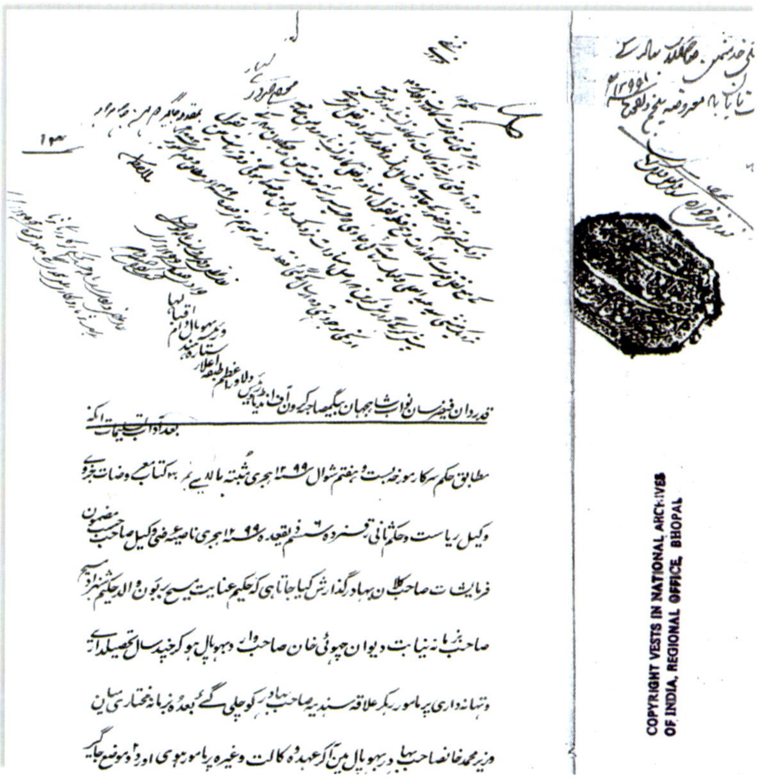

Letter written in 1299 A.H. (1882 AD) giving details of the family history of Bourbons (Page one) Part Translation (after proper address ....
Inayat Masih Bourbon father of Hakim Shahzad Masih Bourbon came to Bhopal during the Diwan ship of Diwan Chote Khan and remained as *Tehsildar* and *Thanedar* for few years and then returned to Gwalior the state of Scindhia. He came back during the time of Wazir Muhammad Khan Bahadur and was appointed to the post of Vikalat, i.e. Political Agency.)

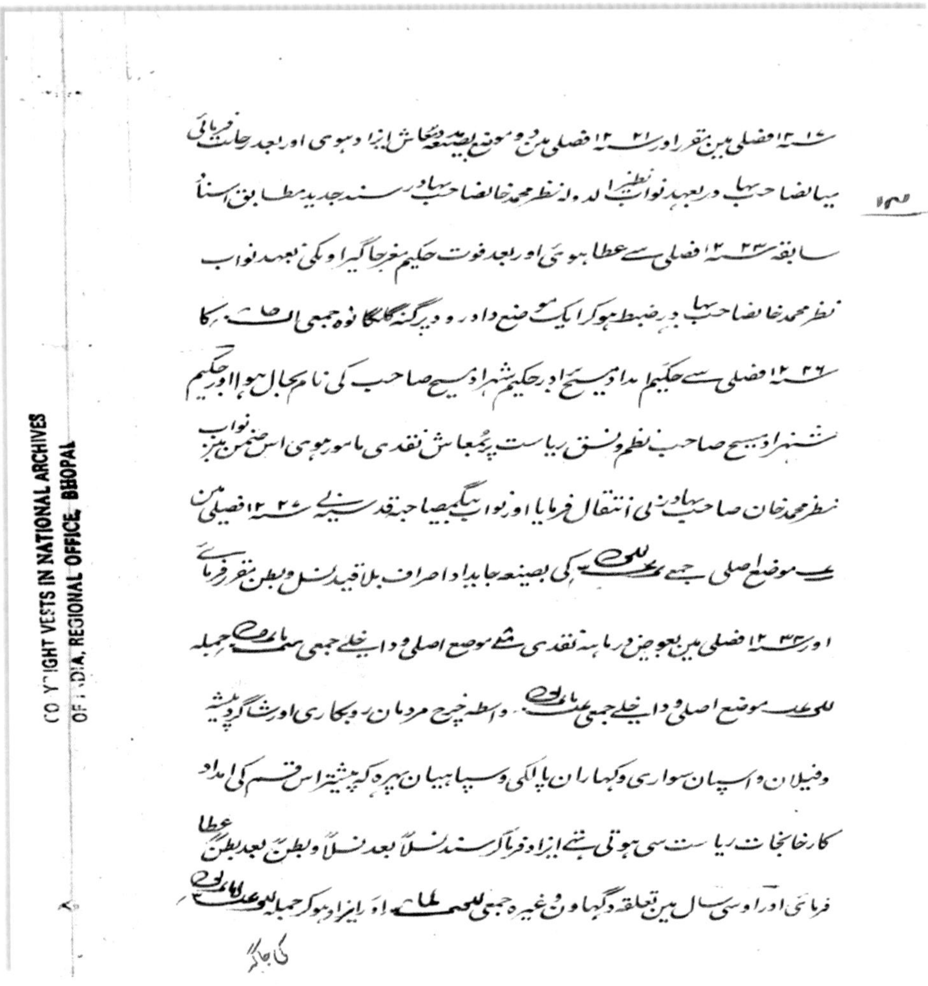

Translation (Shahzad Masih was awarded a Jagir of 2 villages in 1217 Fasli (1228 A.H or 1810 and then 2 more villages in 1812 A.D. for living expenses. It was renewed during the rule of Nazar Mohammad Khan in 1223 Fasli (1817). After his death it was awarded to Hakim Shahzad Masih and Imdad Masih in 1819. Hakim Shahzad Masih became the Prime Minister and after the death of Nazar Mohammad Khan Nawab Qudsia Begum awarded Jagir to meet the expenses of office of Roabkari, Elephants, Horses, Kahars of Palki (palanquin bearers) Policemen, guards, etc.

Chapter 4

BALTHAZAR BOURBON, ALIAS SHAHZAD MASIH

Raisen Treaty 26 February 1818 AD
between
Nawab Nazar Mohammad Khan and East India Company

TREATY between the HONOURABLE the EAST INDIA COMPANY and the NAWAB NUZZUR MAHOMED KHAN, RULER of BHOPAL, concluded by CAPTAIN JOSIAH STEWART on the part of the HONOURABLE COMPANY, in virtue of full powers granted by HIS EXCELLENCY THE MARQUIS OF HASTINGS, K.G., GOVERNOR-GENERAL, ETC., ETC., and by KURRUM MAHOMED KHAN BAHADUR and SHAHZAD MUSSEEH SAHEB on the part of the NAWAB NUZZUR MAHOMED KHAN in virtue of full powers granted by the NAWAB —1818.

ARTICLE 1.

There shall be perpetual friendship, alliance and unity of interests between the Honourable the East India Company and the Nawab of Bhopal, his heirs and successors; and the friends and enemies of one party shall be the friends and enemies of both.

ARTICLE 2.

The British Government engages to guarantee and protect the principality and territory of Bhopal against all enemies.

ARTICLE 3.

The Nawab of Bhopal and his heirs and successors will act in subordinate co-operation with the British Government and acknowledge its supremacy, and will not have any connection with other Chiefs and States.

ARTICLE 4.

The Nawab and his heirs and successors will not enter into negotiation with any Chief or State without the knowledge and sanction of the British Government. But their usual amicable correspondence with friends and relations and necessary correspondence with neighbouring zemindars and managers on matters of small importance shall continue.

ARTICLE 5.

The Nawab and his heirs and successors will not commit aggression on any one. If by accident disputes arise with any one, they shall be submitted to the arbitration and award of the British Government.

ARTICLE 6.

The State of Bhopal shall furnish a contingent of six hundred (600) horse and four hundred (400) infantry for the service of the British Government. Whenever required and when necessary, the whole of the Bhopal forces shall join the British army excepting such a portion as may be requisite for the internal administration of the Country.

ARTICLE 7.

The British troops are to be at all times admitted into the Bhopal territory, the commanding officers of such troops using their utmost endeavour to prevent injury to the crops or other damage, and, if necessary, shall canton there; in which event the Nawab engages, for himself, his heirs and successors, on application to that effect, to cede to the British Government, to serve as a depôt, the fort of Nuzzurghur or of Goolgaon with ground to the distance of 2,000 yards, all round the fort.

ARTICLE 8.

The Nawab, his heirs and successors, will afford every facility to the British troops in obtaining supplies; and all articles of supply required for them shall be purchased in and pass through the Nawab's territory free of duty.

ARTICLE 9.

The Nawab and his heirs and successors shall remain absolute rulers of their country, and the jurisdiction of the British Government shall not in any manner be introduced into that principality.

ARTICLE 10.

The Nawab having exerted himself and employed the resources of his Government with zeal and fidelity in the late service against the Pindarees, the British Government, in order to mark its approbation of his conduct and to enable him to maintain the stipulated contingent hereby grants to the Nawab, his heirs and successors, in perpetuity the five mehals of Ashta, Jehawur, Sehore, Doorahs, and Daveepoora to be held by them in exclusive authority.

ARTICLE 11.

This treaty, consisting of eleven articles having been concluded at Raisen and signed and sealed by Captain Stewart and by Kurrum Mahomed Khan Bahadur and by Shahzad Museeh Saheb, Captain Stewart engages to obtain the ratification of the Governor-General within three weeks from this date; and Kurrum Mahomed Khan and Shahzad Museeh engage to obtain the ratification of the Nawab Nuzzur Mahomed Khan in two days.

Done at Raisen this 26th day of February A.D. 1818, corresponding with the 20th of Rabbee-ul-sanee 1233 of the Hegira.

L. S. (Sd.) J. STEWART.

L. S. (Sd.) KURRUM MAHOMED KHAN.

L. S. (Sd.) SHAHZUD MUSSEEH SAHEB

This Treaty was ratified by His Excellency the Governor-General at Lucknow on the 8th day of March 1818.

Company's Seal. (Sd.) HASTINGS.

Balthazar Bourbon and the Treaty of 1818, with the East India Company

Chapter 5

THE HEROIC ACTS OF MADAM DULHAN AND HER ADOPTED SON, SEBASTIAN BOURBON

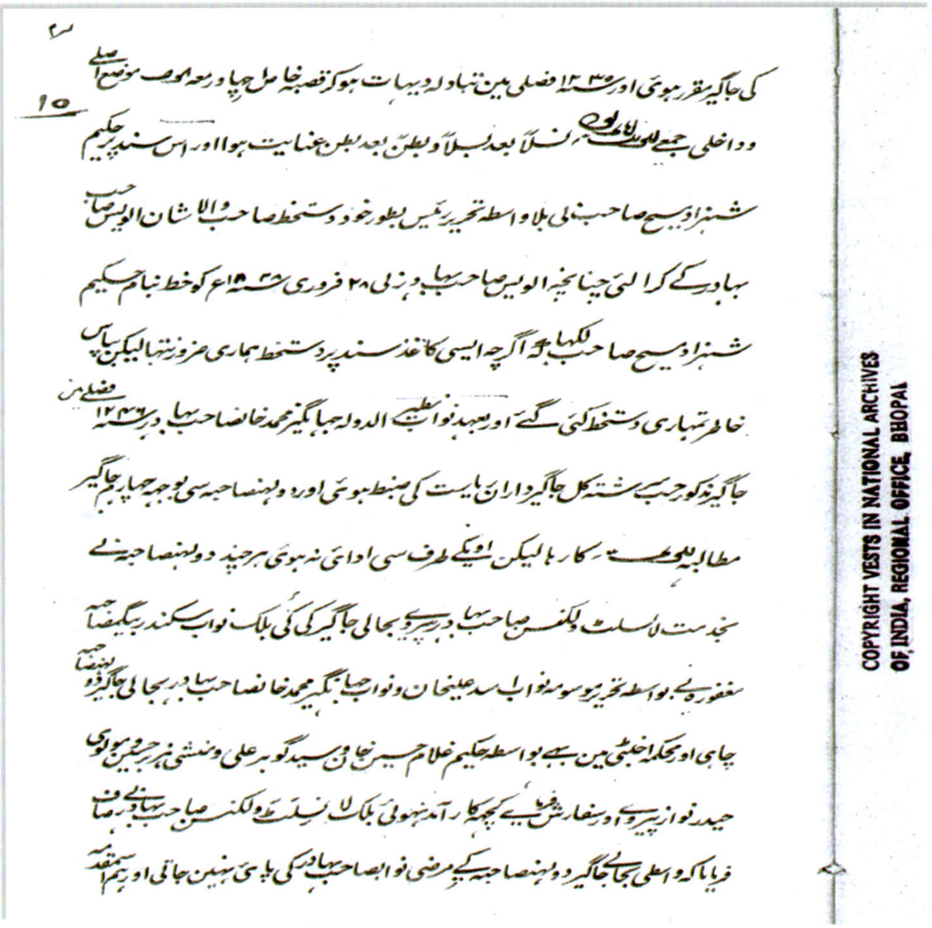

...In 1235 Fasli (1827) regarding Bourbon *jagir* in Ichhawar. Shahzad Masih signed it to send it to Elvis,the political agent. He signed on it on 28th Feb 1828 and also mentioned 'I signed it for you, even though it was not necessary'. During the time of Nawab Jahangir Muhammad Khan it was confiscated from Dulhan Sahib due to non-payment in 1246 Fasli (1840). Dulhan Sahib wrote to Wilkinson, the Political Agent. Sikandar Begum, Hakim Ghulam Husain and Qazi Gouhar Ali and others supported her.

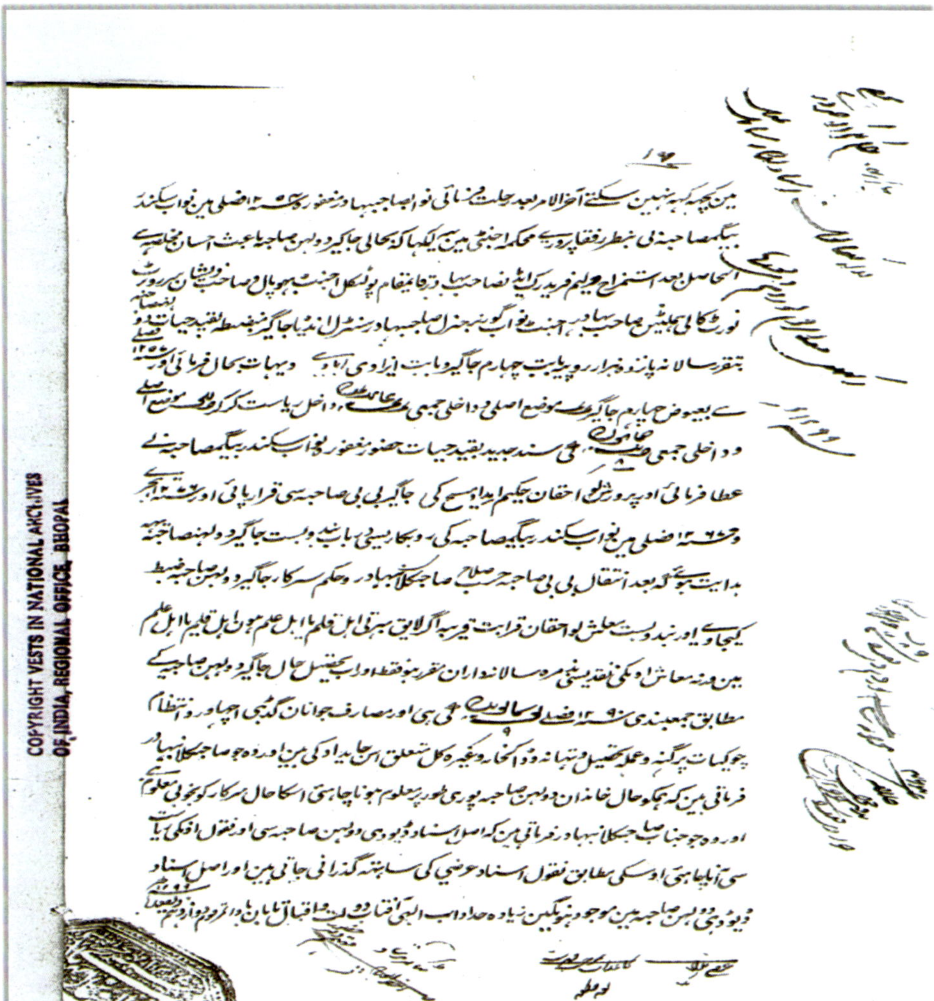

...after the death of Jahangir Muhammad Khan, Nawab Sikandar Begum wrote to the political agent that due to good services rendered by Dulhan Sahib that the *jagir* must be restored....Thus the *jagir* of Dulhan Sahib and agreement was made to the descendants of Imdad Masih in 1267 Fasli 1861...

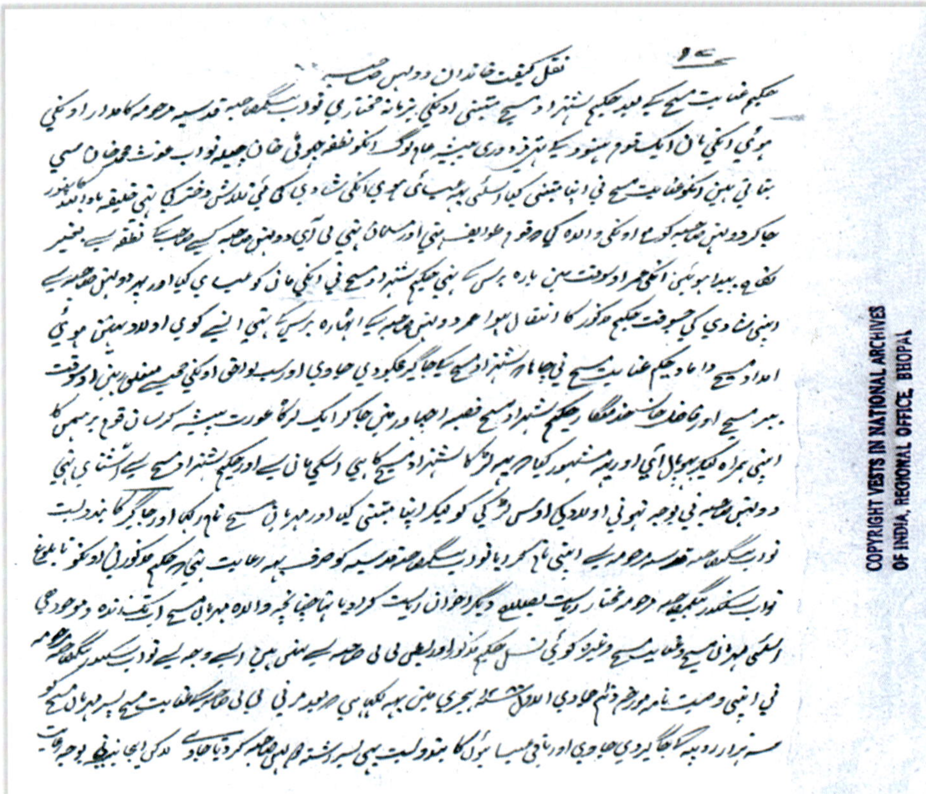

Family of Dulhan Sahib - Translation: After Inayat Masih, his adopted son Hakim Shahzad Masih became the *Kamdar* (Prime minister) of Qudsia Begum. Hakim Shahzad Masih's mother was a Hindu. He was the illegitimate son of Diwan Chote Khan. Inayat Masih adopted him and so he became Christian. For his marriage, Khalifa Bad Allah went to Kanpur and brought along with him Dulhan Sahib and her mother. Dulhan Sahib's mother was a Muslim entertainer and Dulhan Sahib was her illegitimate child. Shahzad Masih accepted Dulhan Sahib to look after his mother. She was twelve at that time. Shahzad Masih married her and when he died she was only 18. She didn't have any children of her own. After Shahzad Masih's death, his uncle Babbar Masih and Fazil Khan brought a boy from Ichhawar to Bhopal. His mother was a Brahmin and told everybody that her child is the son of Shahzad Masih. As there was no son of Shahzad Masih from Dulhan Sahib, she adopted him and named him Meherban Masih (Sebastian Bourbon)

[Note: This could have been written to defame Shahzad Masih and Dulhan Sahib. This was a separate document, not attached to any official signed and sealed file.]

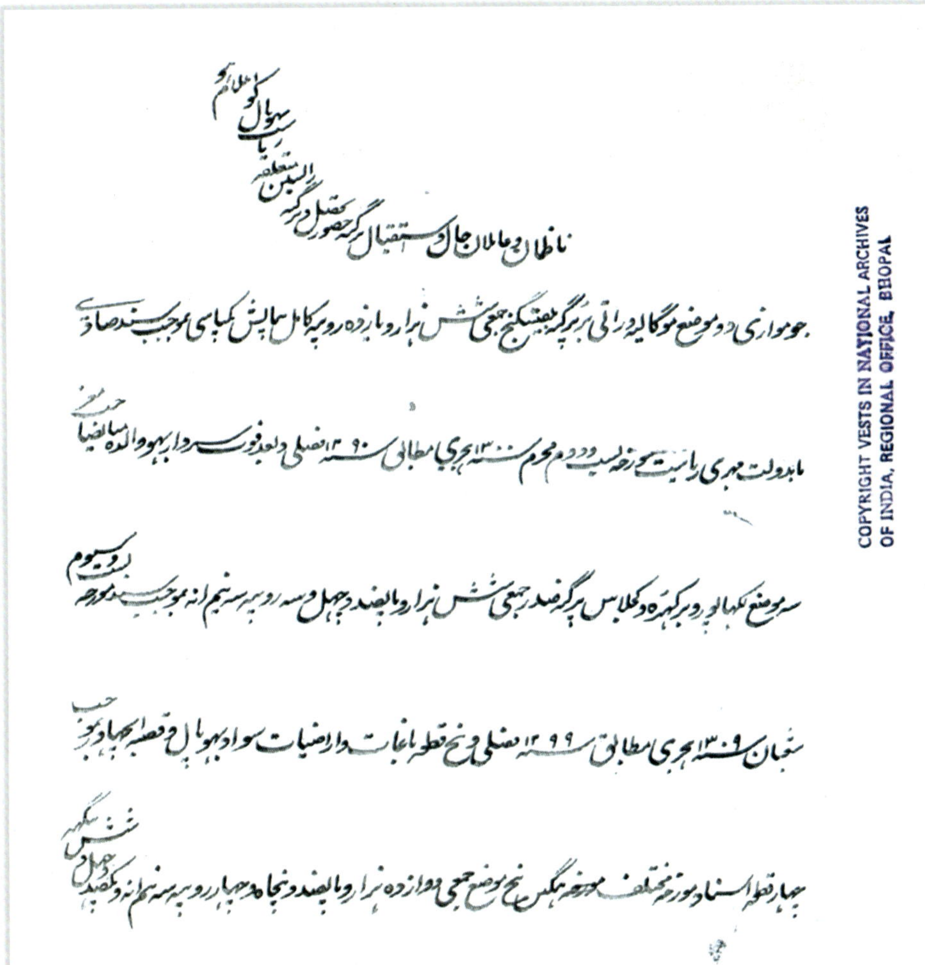

Letter written by Inayat Hussain (page 1, 2, 3) to all the Nazim's officers regarding the order of Nawab Shahjahan Begum on 22 Muharram 1300, 1290 Fasli (1883) Village Lakhapur and Berkhera totalling Rs. 6,543 …5 villages totalling Rs. 22,554; and 146.5 *bigha* garden land was granted to Inayat Masih

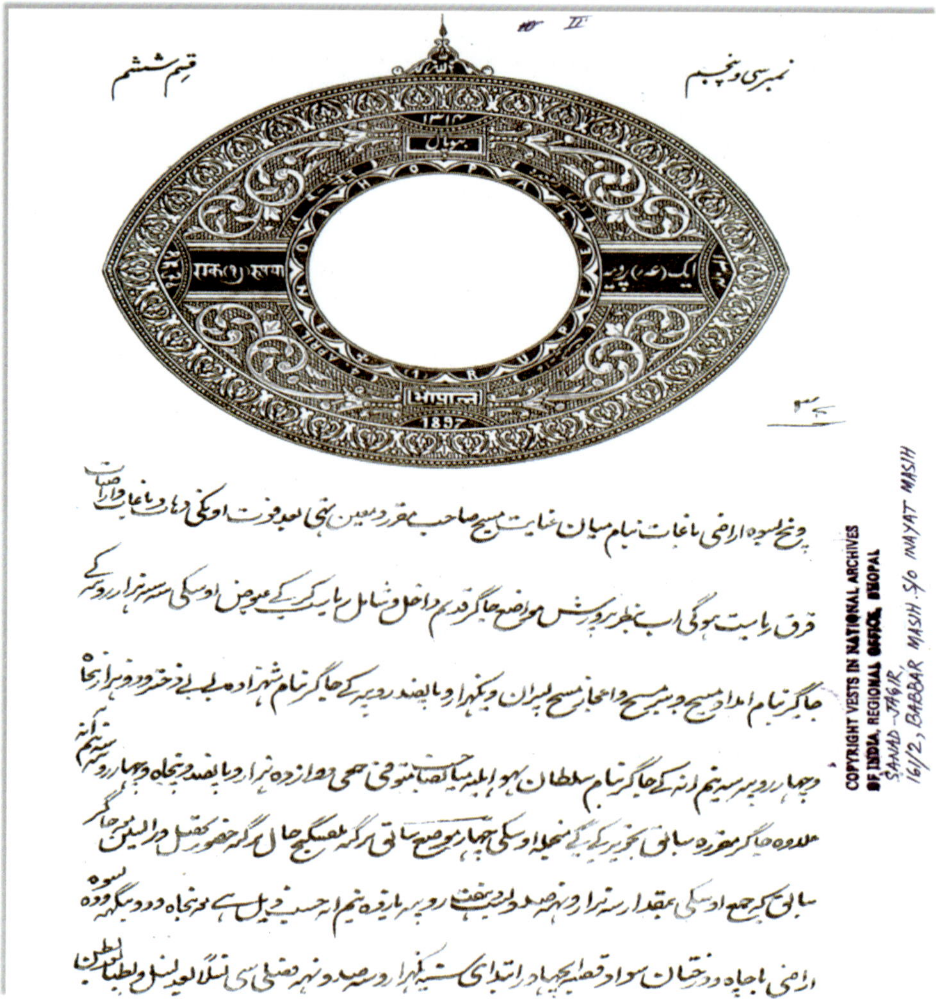

After the death of Inayat Masih, the *jagir*s were confiscated as tradition. Later the *jagir* of Rs. 33,000 was divided between the sons and daughters as follows. Each of the following—Imdad Masih, Babbar Masih and Shahzad Masih got equal share. Further Rs. 1,500 to Shehzadi Bibi who was his daughter. Sultan Bahu wife of Inayat Masih received Rs. 2,054

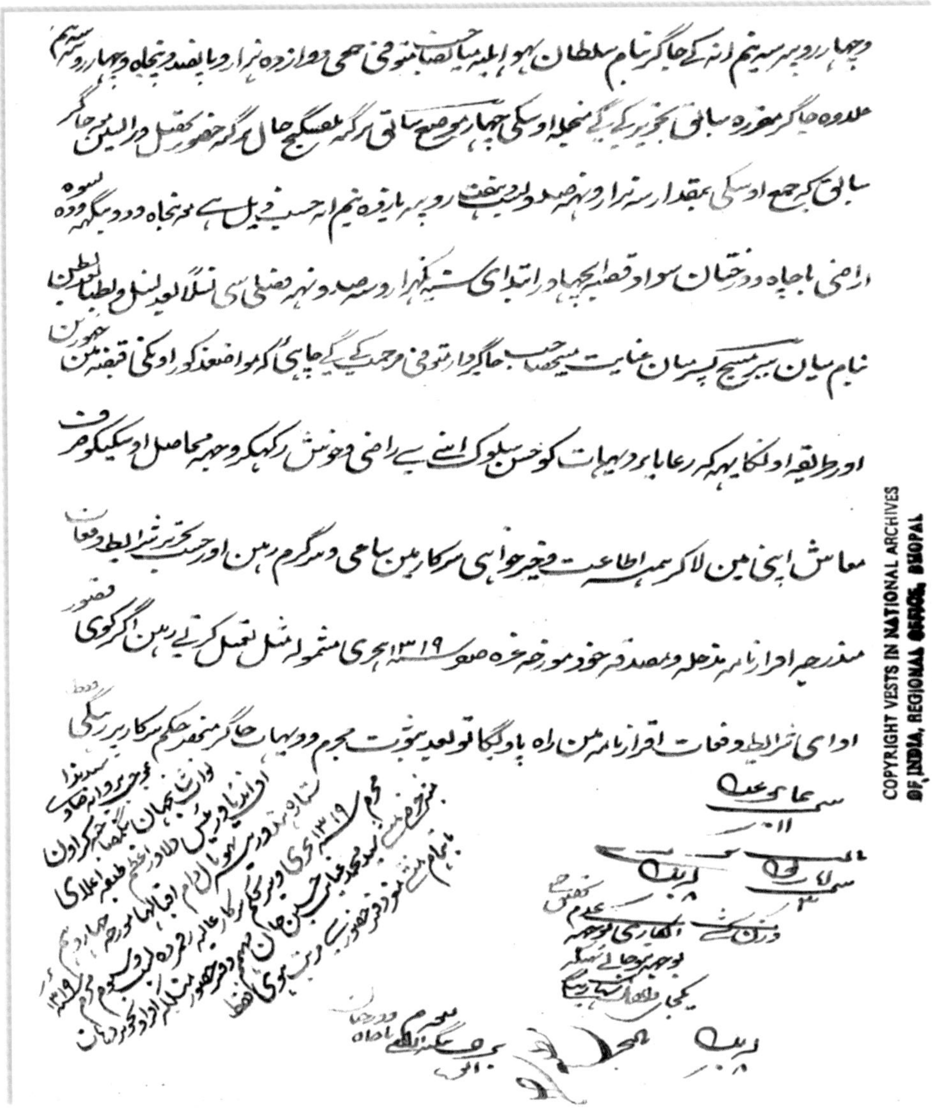

Continuation of letter signed by Syed Muhammad Inayat Husain in charge by the order of Nawab Shahjahan Begum

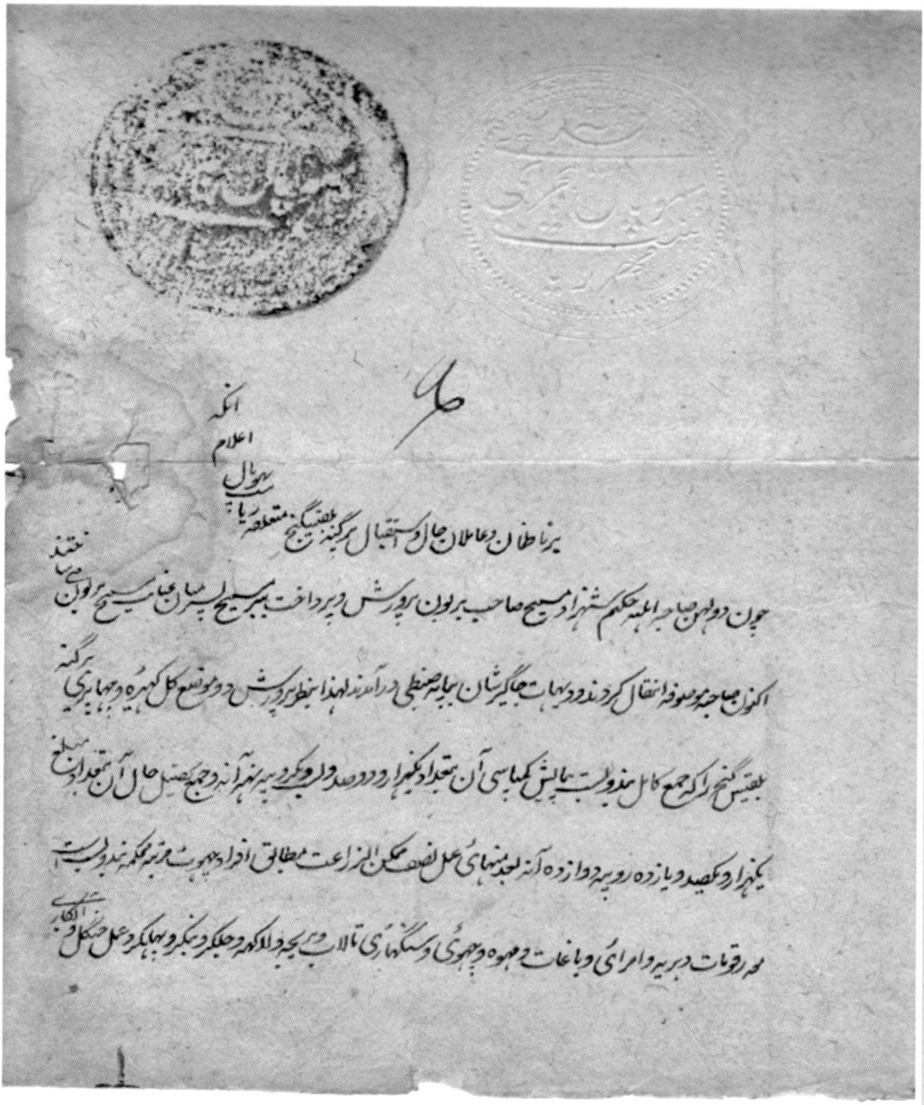

Letter to Nizams regarding renewing *jagir* of Babbar Masih, *jagir* of 2 villages Kulkhera and Jhapri, pargana Bilqisganj

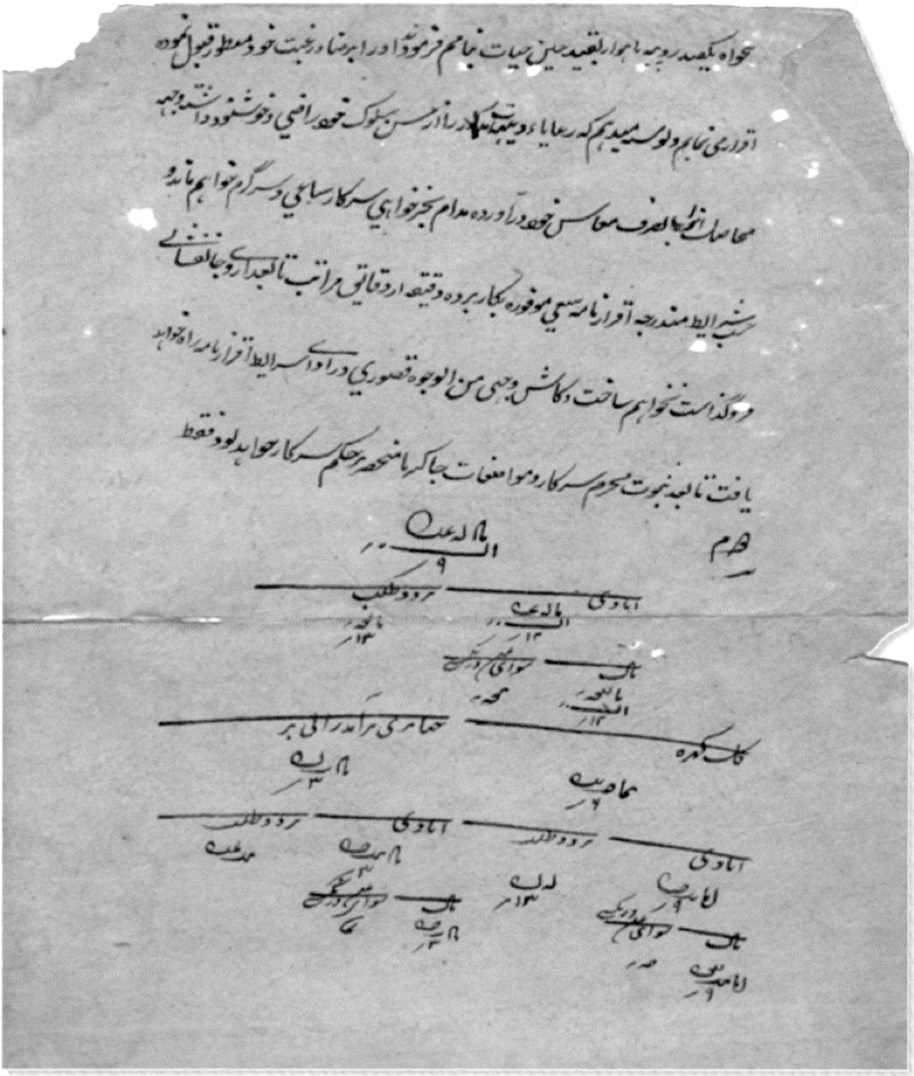

بخواه یکصد روپیه ماهوار بالتعیین حین حیات خاکسار فرمودند و در ابرضا و رغبت خود منظور و قبول نموده

اقرار می نمایم و نوشته میدهیم که رعایا و دیهات ... از حسن سلوک خود راضی و خوشنود داشته بوجه

محاسبات انجا بالطرف معاش خود در آورده مدام بخیرخواهی سرکار سامی و سرگرم خواهیم ماند و

شرایط مندرجه اقرارنامه مسمی موفوره بکار برده دقیقه از دقایق مراتب تا العبداری و جانفشانی

فروگذاشت نخواهیم ساخت و کاشش بوجهی من الوجوه قصوری در ادای شرایط اقرارنامه راه خواهد

یافت تا ابد نبوت محروم سرکار و مواضعات جاگیر با منحصر بحکم سرکار خواهد بود فقط

Application for renewing the land deeds

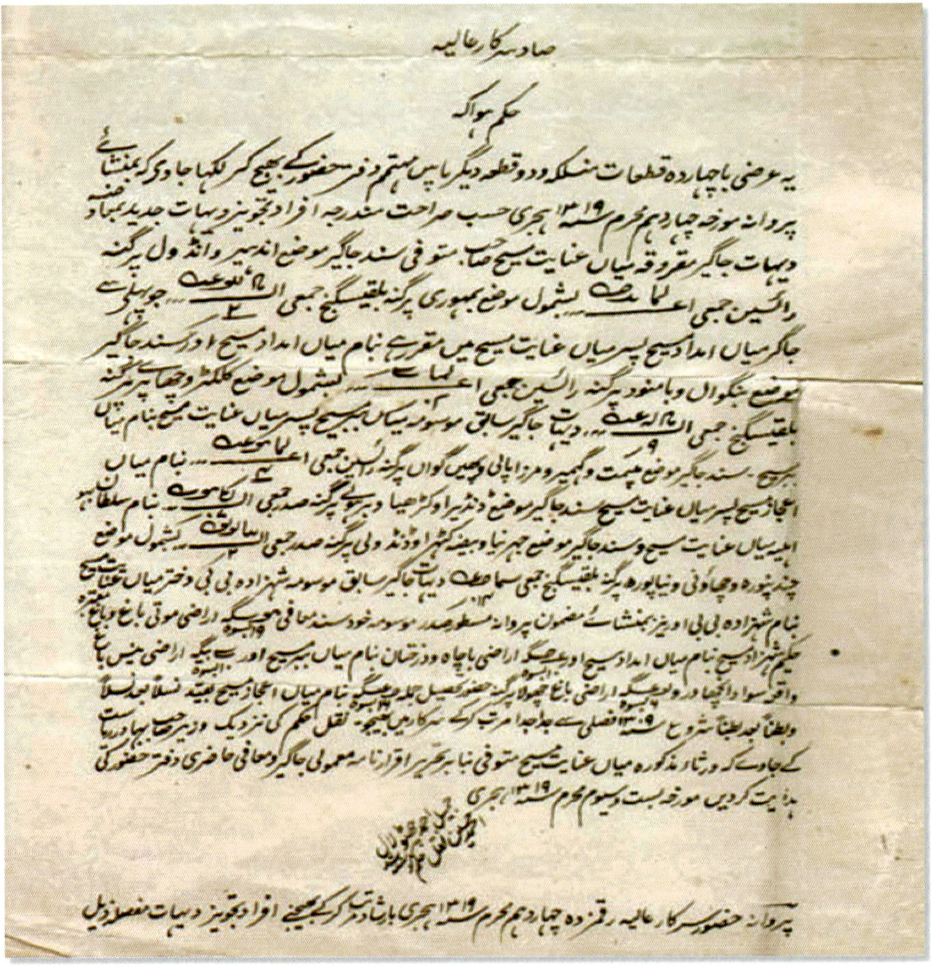

صادرہ سرکار عالیہ

حکم ہوا کہ

Division of Land: By order of Nawab Sultan Jahan Begum dated 14th Muharram 1319 A.H. (03 May 1901) allotment of *jagir* of Andser, Andol, of Pargana Raisen, and Bamohri Pargana Bilqisganj, which were already *jagir*s of Imdad Masih, son of Inayat Masih were renewed and granted to Imdad Masih. Bangwan and Bangmod Pargana Raisen and Collector and Chapripargana Bilqisganj *jagir* of Babbar Masih to Babbar Masih son of Inayat Masih.......To Aijaz Masih .... To Sultan Bahu...... to Shehzadi Bibi....... Moti Bagh and Bagh Maqbara Sharif Shahzad Masih to Imdad Masih and Well or Baoli with trees to Babbar Masih.... To Aijaz Masih.

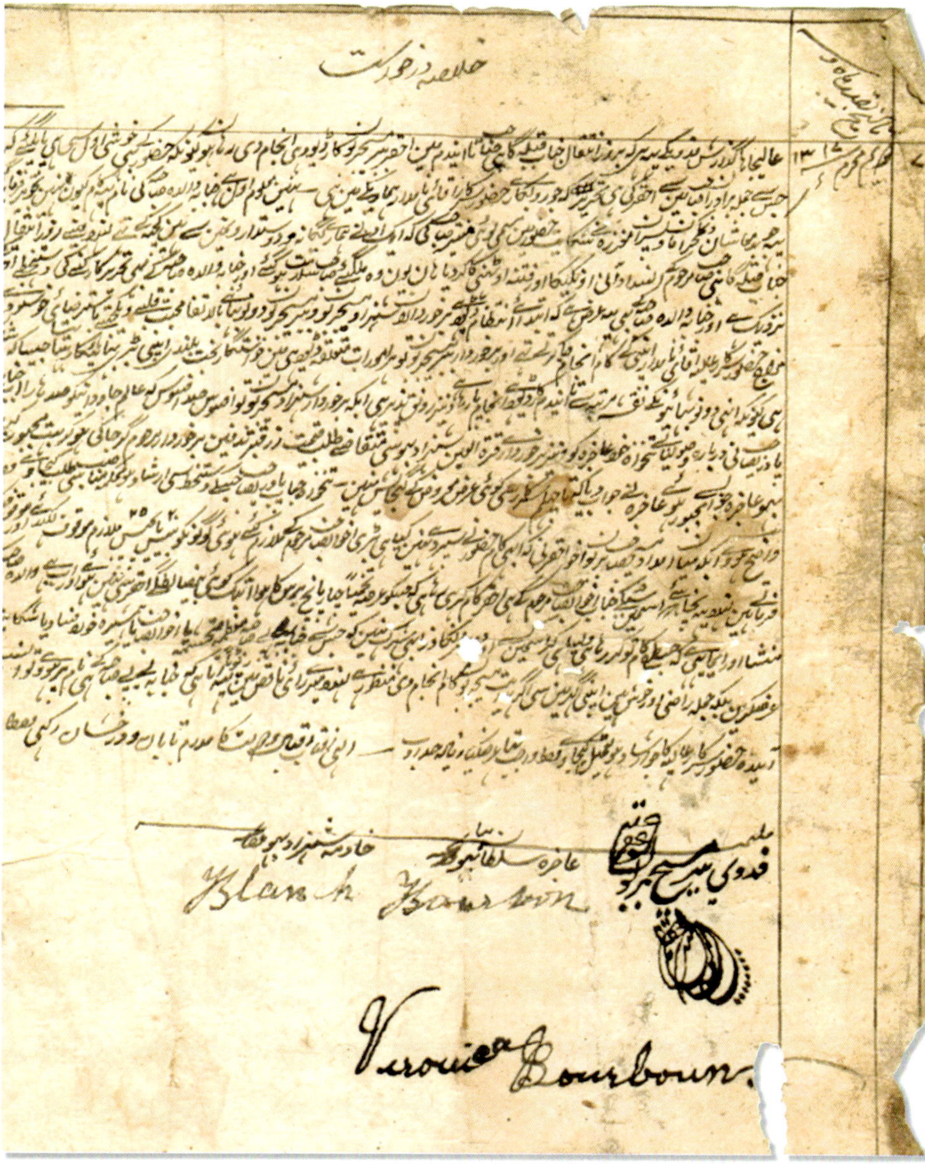

Application given by the family regarding distribution of *jagir* (Property) 2nd Muharram 1317 (13 May 1899)

Chapter 9

MAGDALINE BOURBON

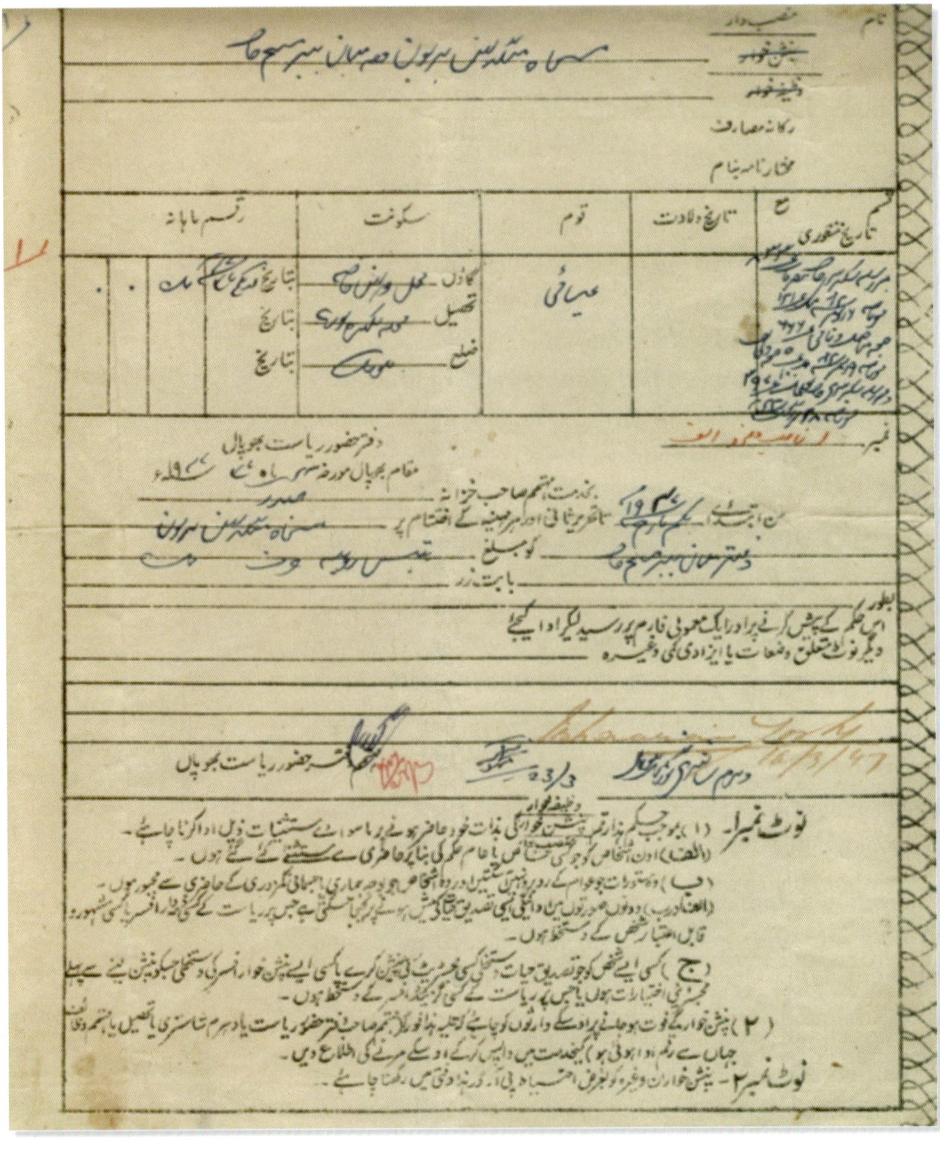

Letter dated 01 March 1947 addressed to Magdaline Bourbon, regarding *mansab* (pension) of Rs. 30. The address was Dulhan Sahiba Mahal at Lakherapura.

Letter of approval of the Pension or *mansab* grant of the amount Rs. 30 to Magdaline Bourbon. Approval dated 16 May 1912. At that time she was studying in Lalbagh, Lucknow.

Chapter 10

THE FAMILY TREE OF THE BOURBONS IN INDIA AND THE LATER BOURBONS

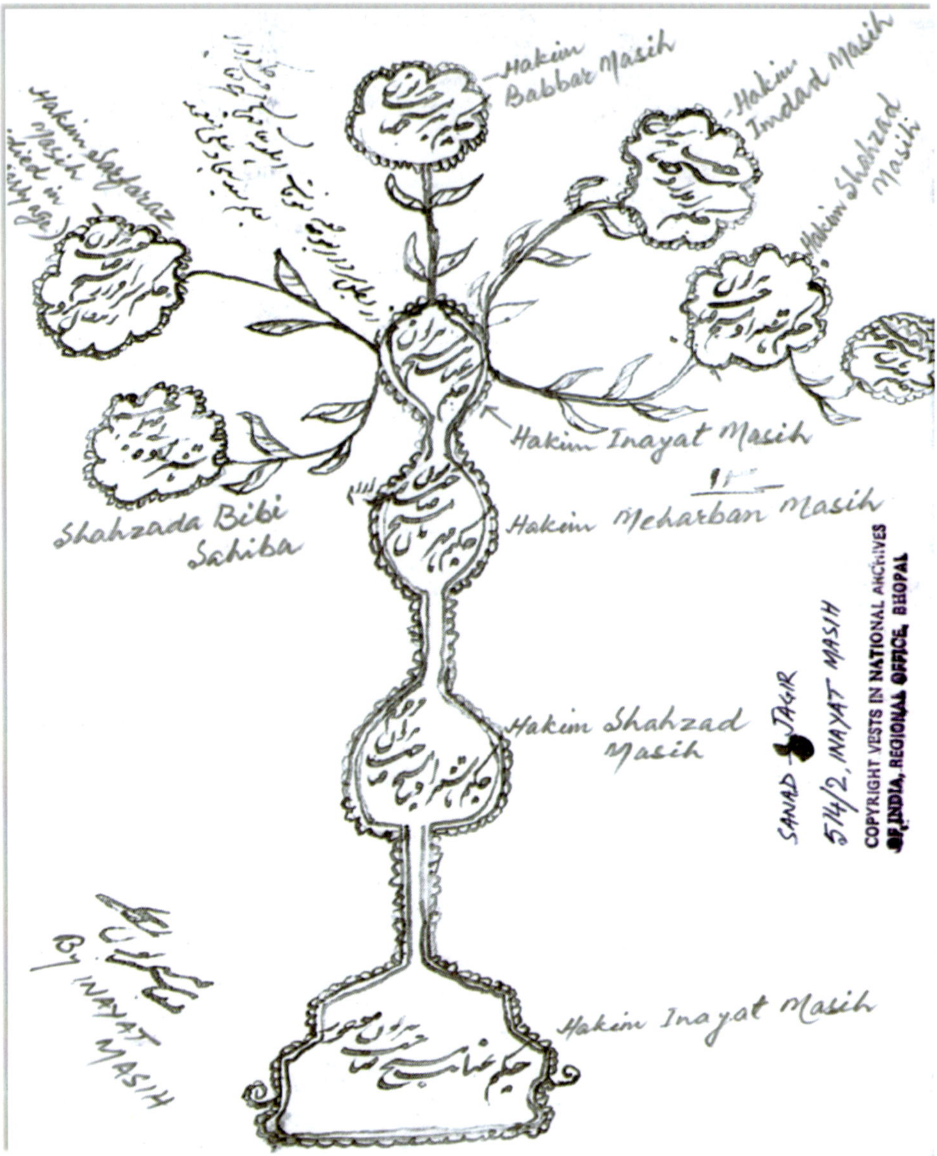

Bourbon family tree recovered from National Archives

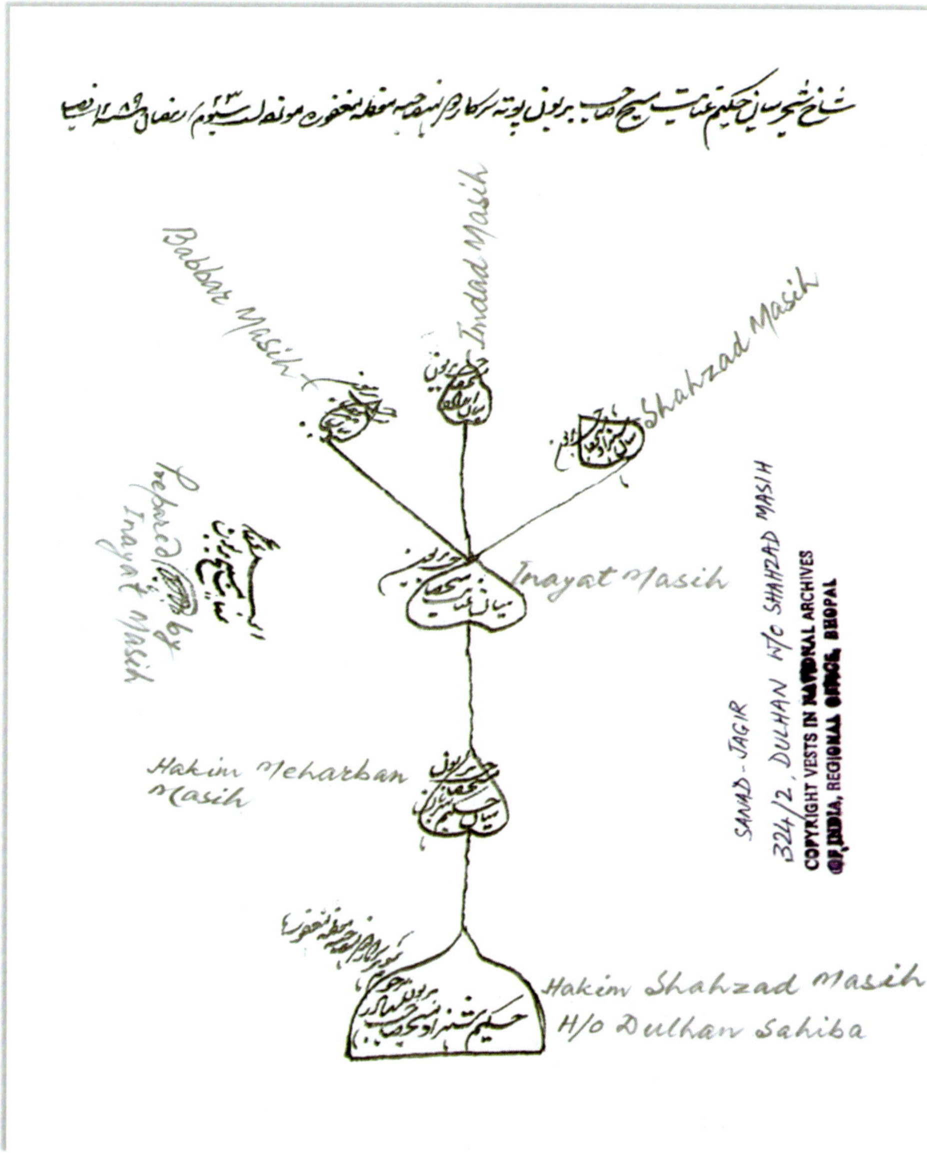

Bourbon family tree recovered from National Archives

ACKNOWLEDGEMENTS

There have been numerous well-wishers for this book. I will not do justice if I mention just a few. I thank all my friends who have supported and encouraged me to write. I would like to thank my family members, including my daughters Radhika Iyengar, Pooja Iyengar and Shabnam Malhotra for giving me inspiration, and for their patience and support. I am also thankful to my sister Sushiela for rendering me all possible assistance and discussions, including refreshing the memories and stories as told by my mother Magdaline Bourbon.

My research help came from Mrs Pranjana Sinha and Mumtaz Baig Sahab at National Archives, Regional office Bhopal and State Archives. They have spent countless hours with me to locate old documents and photographs. The Catholic Archdiocese in Bhopal and in Agra helped to validate the birth and death dates of the Bourbon family with their baptism and death records. St. Francis Church Jehangirabad, Bhopal, and Church of Agra were my two major sources for dates. I am grateful to the Archbishop of Bhopal, Leo Cornelio, for his permission to access the church archives.

I must not forget to thank Mohammad Sulaiman Khan (Acche Sahib) and his sons Mohammad Irfan Khan and

Muhammad Rizwan Khan for providing a great deal of valuable information regarding the family tree. This book has helped me to look at Bhopal from a photographical and a historical lens. Abdul Mujeeb Farooqui, a renowned photojournalist in Bhopal ventured into old buildings and captured their beauty with his lens. I would also like to thank S.M. Husain Sahab, an architect by profession for his comments on French architecture. A special note of thanks to Uttam for his help to dig out old books at Bhopal's Central Library.

Last, but not the least, I would like to thank Rizwan Uddin Ansari who spent considerable time fact-checking and validating the claims made in this book. His help was also critical in finding the location of the graves of the Bourbon family in Bhopal. He helped with Urdu translations as well.

I have mainly used photographs that I possessed from my mother. I have also used some publicly available photographs, to supplement Bhopal's history and have not been able to trace their original sources. Thus I would like thank all those people, whose pictures I have used in this book.

INDEX

Note: The names of the Bourbons appear as 'First name Surname', while all other names appear as 'Surname, First name'.